The
Practical Grammar Handbook
for College Writers

The
Practical Grammar Handbook
for College Writers

Marian Anders

Carolina Academic Press
Durham, North Carolina

Library of Congress Cataloging-in-Publication Data

Practical grammar handbook for college writers / Marian Anders.
  p. cm.
  Includes bibliographical references and index.
  ISBN 978-1-61163-168-5 (alk. paper)
  1. English language--Grammar. 2. English language--Rhetoric. 3. Report writing. I. Title.

PE1112.A54 2012
428.2--dc23   2012012691

Carolina Academic Press
700 Kent Street
Durham, NC 27701
Telephone (919) 489-7486
Fax (919) 493-5668
www.cap-press.com

Printed in the United States of America

Contents

Contents

Contents

Contents

Contents

Introduction

As a student, I always enjoyed English and got good grades, but I didn't understand grammar. I had a natural talent for language and writing, so I got good grades on my papers without really knowing what I was doing.

I began learning grammar when I was working on my Master's degree in English at Florida State University. When I became a teacher and saw how frustrated my students got, I started developing my practical grammar approach which presents the material step-by-step in a logical fashion and provides a variety of tricks for students to use.

I have taught English grammar, composition, and literature to college freshmen and sophomores for twenty years, and the methods presented in this handbook work for all kinds of students, those who love writing and those who find it difficult. These methods work because they are based on logic rather than memorizing rules or lists of words.

My students have told me, "I always hated English, but this isn't too bad," and "I never understood grammar before, but this makes it easy." *The Practical Grammar Handbook for College Writers* focuses on what you need to know and explains everything quickly and clearly. Grammar may never be your favorite subject, but it doesn't have to be a mystery either.

—Marian Anders

About the Author

Marian Anders earned a Master of Arts degree in English from Florida State University. She has twenty years' experience teaching all levels of grammar and composition, from basic skills developmental to advanced college grammar. She teaches English at Alamance Community College in Graham, North Carolina.

Acknowledgments

I offer my thanks and appreciation to the many English teachers I have had the privilege of working with for the past twenty years. By sharing ideas and supporting each other, we have all become better teachers. I especially thank Jeannie Murphy, my friend and mentor from Pierce College, who taught me the intricacies of traditional grammar, and to Nancy Bolle, also from Pierce College, who was a supportive friend when I was a new teacher.

Abundant thanks also to my family for their invaluable support.

This book is dedicated to all my students—past, present, and future.

The
Practical Grammar Handbook
for College Writers

Chapter One

Verbs and Subjects

Most people have learned to find the subject of a sentence by asking, "What is the sentence about?" To find the verb, most people have been told, "Look for an action word." Sometimes that method works, but often it doesn't.

> She enjoys baking brownies.

What is this sentence about? Most people would say *brownies*. What is the action word? Most people would say *baking*. But the subject of this sentence is not *brownies*; it's *she*. And the verb is not *baking*; it's *enjoys*.

In this chapter you will learn to find the verb first and then the subject by using a method that always works.

Take your time on this chapter because everything you need to know about grammar builds on your ability to find the verb and the subject.

Finding Verbs

Most people were taught to find the verb in a sentence by looking for the action word. Sometimes that method works, but other times it doesn't. The **time change** method is much easier, and best of all, it always works.

Change the time of the sentence by saying *yesterday, every day,* and *tomorrow* at the beginning of the sentence. When you change the time of the sentence, the verb will change automatically.

Listen for the word (or words) that changes when you change the time. That word is the verb.

> *Yesterday* Steve **ATE** a pizza. (past)
> *Every day* Steve **EATS** a pizza. (present)
> *Tomorrow* Steve **WILL EAT** a pizza. (future)

> *Yesterday* Jill **BOUGHT** a new pair of shoes.
> *Every day* Jill **BUYS** a new pair of shoes.
> *Tomorrow* Jill **WILL BUY** a new pair of shoes.

Try these sentences on your own and then check your answers below.

> My dog bites the English teacher.
> *Yesterday* My dog . . .
> *Every day* My dog . . .
> *Tomorrow* My dog . . .

Here are the answers:

> *Yesterday* My dog **BIT** the English teacher.
> *Every day* My dog bites the English teacher. (no change)
> *Tomorrow* My dog **WILL BITE** the English teacher.

In the *every day* sentence, nothing changed because the original sentence was already in the present. The verb changes when you change the time. The word *bites* changed, so *bites* is the verb.

Now try this one and check your answers below:

> My brother Charlie got a flat tire.
> *Yesterday* My brother Charlie . . .
> *Every day* My brother Charlie . . .
> *Tomorrow* My brother Charlie . . .

Here are the answers:

> *Yesterday* My brother Charlie got a flat tire.
> *Every day* My brother Charlie **GETS** a flat tire.
> *Tomorrow* My brother Charlie **WILL GET** a flat tire.

This time the *yesterday* sentence didn't change because the original sentence was already in the past. The word *got* changed, so *got* is the verb.

So when you change the time to find the verb, use all three time words; the verb will change with two of them.

Getting tricky . . .

You may have heard the terms **action verb**, **linking verb**, and **helping verb**.

For practical grammar, all that matters is, "Does this sentence have a verb, yes or no?" The kind of verb doesn't matter, and changing the time always works for finding every kind of verb.

If you want to learn more, turn to **Types of Verbs** on page 211.

Let's try some tricky sentences. Remember, don't look for the verb. Listen for the word that changes.

> Jackie loves playing volleyball.
> *Yesterday* Jackie **LOVED** playing volleyball.
> *Every day* Jackie loves playing volleyball.
> *Tomorrow* Jackie **WILL LOVE** playing volleyball.

The word that changed is *loves*, so *loves* is the verb.

Are you surprised that *playing* wasn't the verb? *Playing* looks like an action word, but it did not change when we changed the time. The real verb will always change.

> **Getting tricky . . .**
>
> If **playing** isn't the verb, what is it?
>
> **Playing** is a **direct object**. See page 221.

Try finding the verb in these sentences and then check your answers below:

> Susan enjoyed jogging in the park.
> *Yesterday* Susan . . .
> *Every day* Susan . . .
> *Tomorrow* Susan . . .

> Mark wants to win the trophy.
> *Yesterday* Mark . . .
> *Every day* Mark . . .
> *Tomorrow* Mark . . .

Here are the answers:

> Susan enjoyed jogging in the park.
> *Yesterday* Susan enjoyed jogging in the park.
> *Every day* Susan **ENJOYS** jogging in the park.
> *Tomorrow* Susan **WILL ENJOY** jogging in the park.

The verb is the word that changed: *enjoyed*. Why isn't *jogging* the verb? *Jogging* didn't change when we changed the time.

> Mark wants to win the race.
> *Yesterday* Mark **WANTED** to win the race.
> *Every day* Mark wants to win the race.
> *Tomorrow* Mark **WILL WANT** to win the race.

The verb is the word that changed: *wants*. Why isn't *win* the verb? *Win* didn't change when we changed the time.

The verb is always the word that changes.

Getting tricky . . .

If **jogging** and **win** aren't verbs, what are they?

Jogging and **to win** are both **direct objects**.

See page 221.

Jogging is also a **gerund**, page 215.

To win is also an **infinitive**, page 215.

Sentences with more than one Verb

A sentence can have more than one verb. When you change the time, all the verbs in the sentence will change.

> The garden will look beautiful and smell heavenly.
>
> *Yesterday* The garden **LOOKED** beautiful and **SMELLED** heavenly.
>
> *Every day* The garden **LOOKS** beautiful and **SMELLS** heavenly.

If the sentence is long, it can be useful to say the time word again in the middle.

> Gloria washed the dishes, and Bob dried them.
>
> *Every day* Gloria **WASHES** the dishes, and *every day* Bob **DRIES** them.
>
> *Tomorrow* Gloria **WILL WASH** the dishes, and *tomorrow* Bob **WILL DRY** them.

Exercise 1.1 Finding Verbs

Say *yesterday, every day, and tomorrow* at the beginning of each sentence and listen for the words that change. Some sentences have one verb and others have two. Mark the verbs with a <u>double underline</u>.

Check your answers on page 237.

1. My neighbor George loves gardening.

2. Every weekend he works in his yard.

3. George went on-line and ordered six apple trees.

4. The trees came in the mail in a large cardboard box; they were only three feet tall.

5. George sweated profusely as he dug six holes in his yard.

6. Blisters stung his hands, yet he continued working.

7. Then he shoveled compost into each hole.

8. After planting the trees, George firmed the soil around their roots.

9. Soon the little trees will bloom, and the blossoms will look so pretty.

10. In only four years, George will harvest his first apples.

Exercise 1.2 Finding Verbs

Say *yesterday, every day,* and *tomorrow* at the beginning of each sentence and listen for the words that change. Some sentences have one verb and others have two. Mark the verbs with a <u>double underline</u>.

Check your answers on page 238.

1. Video games are a multi-billion dollar industry.

2. Many people think that *Pong* was the first video game.

3. *Pong* comes from the game of table tennis; in *Pong* players slide the paddles back and forth to hit the ball.

4. Although *Pong* was not the first video game, its success took the video game industry mainstream.

5. Earlier video games included *Spacewar* and *Chase;* *Chase* was first video game for television.

6. Some teachers even use computer games to teach their students.

7. Programs allow students to play a game after they master a new concept.

8. Typing programs often include games to improve typing speed.

9. Even some museums use video games as part of their displays such as the stock trading simulation game at the Chicago Board of Trade Museum.

10. After finishing these sentences, you will reward yourself and play your favorite video game.

Finding Subjects

When you analyze a sentence, always find the verb first. Then you can find the subject by asking yourself, "Who or what performed the verb?"

> Janisa baked a peach pie.
> *Tomorrow* Janisa **WILL BAKE** a peach pie.
> *Every day* Janisa **BAKES** a peach pie.

The verb is *baked.* To find the subject, ask yourself, "Who or what baked a peach pie?"

The answer, of course, is *Janisa.* Mark subjects with a <u>single underline</u>.

> <u>Janisa</u> <u>baked</u> a peach pie.

Were you tempted to mark *pie* as the subject? Ask yourself, "Did the pie bake anything?" No, Janisa baked it, so the subject is *Janisa.*

> ## Getting tricky . . .
>
> If **pie** isn't the subject, what is it?
>
> **Pie** is a **direct object**. See page 221.

In most sentences, the subject comes before the verb. The subject can come after the verb, but that doesn't happen too often.

> ## Getting tricky . . .
>
> For examples of sentences in which the subject comes after the verb, see pages 216–219.

Sentences with more than one Subject

Katie and Jake <u>swim</u> at the YMCA.

The verb is *swim*. To find the subject, ask yourself, "Who or what swims at the YMCA?" Katie and Jake both swim. They are two subjects sharing one verb, so underline both names:

<u>Katie</u> and <u>Jake</u> <u>swim</u> at the YMCA.

A sentence can have several verbs and several subjects.

> Gloria <u>washed</u> the dishes, and Bob <u>dried</u> them.

Ask the subject question for each verb. "Who or what washed the dishes?" *Gloria* washed the dishes. "Who or what dried them?" *Bob* dried them.

Underline both subjects:

> <u>Gloria</u> <u>washed</u> the dishes, and <u>Bob</u> <u>dried</u> them.

Here's a harder one:

> After he <u>mowed</u> the lawn, Andre <u>took</u> a shower, and then he <u>watched</u> TV.

Ask the subject question for each verb, and remember that the subject will usually come before its verb. "Who or what mowed the lawn?" *He* mowed the lawn. "Who or what took a shower? *Andre* took a shower. "Who or what watched tv?" *He* watched TV.

Underline all the subjects:

> After <u>he</u> <u>mowed</u> the lawn, <u>Andre</u> <u>took</u> a shower, and then <u>he</u> <u>watched</u> TV.

> ### Getting tricky . . .
>
> The subject of the sentence will either be a
> **noun** or **pronoun**. For an explanation of nouns
> and pronouns, see page 229.

One Word Subjects

Usually it's best to underline just one word for each subject.

> My brother is a scuba instructor.

"Who or what is a scuba instructor?" *My brother.*

If you want to underline only one word, which word would you choose? *Brother* is a better choice than *my.*

> My <u>brother</u> is a scuba instructor.

Here's another example:

> Jessica's room is messy.

"Who or what is messy?" *Jessica's room.*

Which one word would you choose? Is *Jessica* messy? Maybe she is, but that's not what the sentence is about. Is the *room* messy? Yes.

> Jessica's <u>room</u> is messy.

But if the subject is a person's name, underline the entire name:

> <u>Dr. Martin Luther King, Jr.</u>, <u>gave</u> his famous speech in 1963.

Now here is a tricky one:

> My favorite ride at Disney World <u>is</u> the Haunted Mansion.

"Who or what is the Haunted Mansion?" *Disney World* is the Haunted Mansion? No.

How about *my favorite ride* is the Haunted Mansion? Yes, but that's three words. Which one word would you choose? *Ride* is the best choice.

My favorite <u>ride</u> at Disney World <u>is</u> the Haunted Mansion.

Strange Subjects

Don't get confused if the subject is a word that looks like a verb. In grammar, we don't care what a word looks like. We only care about the job it is doing in the sentence. The job of a subject is to tell who or what performed the verb.

> Dancing <u>is</u> fun.

"Who or what is fun?" *Dancing* is fun. Underline the subject:

> <u>Dancing</u> <u>is</u> fun.

Here is a tricky sentence:

Cleaning the bathroom is disgusting.

"Who or what is disgusting?" *Cleaning the bathroom* is disgusting. Which one word would you choose? Is the *bathroom* disgusting? It might be, but this sentence is about *cleaning* the bathroom. Underline the subject:

Cleaning the bathroom is disgusting.

> ### Getting tricky . . .
>
> **Dancing** and **cleaning** are subjects, and they are also both **gerunds**. For an explanation of gerunds, see page 215.

Exercise 1.3 Finding Subjects

Double underline the verbs. Some sentences have one verb; others have two. Then, to find the subject, ask "Who or what performed the verb?" Some sentences have one subject; others have two or three. Underline just one word for each subject. Check your answers on page 239.

1. Professor Smith's literature class will study poetry.

2. The registrar spent two days fixing the schedules after the college's computer system crashed.

3. England established the first toll roads in 1269.

4. Dylan's favorite breakfast food is cold pizza.

5. Consumers in the United States discard nearly one hundred million cell phones annually.

6. Tiffany and Erika will work at Burger King this summer; Jasmine will serve as a camp counselor.

7. Sharing an apartment requires compromise.

8. Many people use the internet to reserve hotel rooms.

9. Germany and Japan recycle more than eighty percent of the glass and paper used in their countries.

Exercise 1.4 Finding Subjects

Double underline the verbs. Some sentences have one verb; others have two. Then, to find the subject, ask, "Who or what performed the verb?" Some sentences have one subject; others have two or three. Underline just one word for each subject. Check your answers on page 240.

1. Jeremy bought a new phone last week.

2. His old phone always dropped calls.

3. Melissa and Kari made an inexpensive desk out of a wooden door and two small file cabinets.

4. Friction between the brake pads and the wheel rims on a bicycle creates a bicycle's braking action.

5. On the day before Christmas, tape, scissors, and wrapping paper cluttered the dining room table.

6. Alonzo first finished his calculus homework, and then he started his research paper on Napoleon.

7. In the 1960s Eartha Kitt and Cesar Romero made guest appearances on the *Batman* television series.

8. Chandra and Francis planned to go shopping, but their car's battery was dead.

9. After his computer crashed, Joseph tried writing his paper by hand.

10. When he got a cramp in his hand, Joseph went next door and borrowed his neighbor's laptop.

Chapter Two

Phrases, Independent Clauses, and Dependent Clauses

In this chapter you will learn two essential things:

1. the difference between a clause and a phrase

2. the difference between an independent clause and a dependent clause

Phrases, dependent clauses, and independent clauses are the building blocks that we use to make sentences. When you understand the difference between them, you will have the foundation for everything that comes next.

Clauses and Phrases

A **clause** is a group of words that has a subject and a verb.

A **phrase** is a group of words that doesn't have a subject and a verb.

We put clauses and phrases together to make sentences of different lengths. A very short sentence has just one clause. A very long sentence could have several clauses and several phrases.

To determine whether a group of words is a clause or a phrase, just look for a verb and a subject:

> The world's smallest dog is a Chihuahua

Look for a verb by changing the time of the sentence:

> *Yesterday* The world's smallest dog **WAS** a Chihuahua
>
> *Tomorrow* The world's smallest dog **WILL BE** a Chihuahua

Double underline the word that changes:

> The world's smallest dog <u>is</u> a Chihuahua

Now look for a subject. "Who or what is a Chihuahua? *The world's smallest dog* is a Chihuahua. Which one word would you choose? *Dog.* Underline the subject:

> The world's smallest <u>dog</u> <u>is</u> a Chihuahua

This group of words is a **clause** because it has a subject and a verb.

Now try this one:

> Lives in Kentucky

Look for a verb by changing the time:

> *Yesterday* **LIVED** in Kentucky.
> *Tomorrow* **WILL LIVE** in Kentucky.

Double underline the verb:

> <u>Lives</u> in Kentucky

Now look for a subject. "Who or what lives in Kentucky?" It doesn't say. This group of words doesn't have a subject, so it is not a clause; it's a **phrase**.

Here's one more example:

> Only four inches tall at the shoulders

Look for a verb by changing the time:

> *Yesterday* Only four inches tall at the shoulders
> *Every day* Only four inches tall at the shoulders
> *Tomorrow* Only four inches tall at the shoulders

Nothing changed. This group of words does not have a verb. It's a **phrase.** We don't need to bother looking for a subject. A clause needs a subject and a verb. If a group of words doesn't have a verb, it must be a phrase.

Exercise 2.1 Identifying Clauses and Phrases

Step 1)   Change the time and listen for a verb. If you find a verb, <u>double</u> <u>underline</u> it.
If there is no verb, mark Ph for phrase, and you're finished with that one.

Step 2)   If you have a verb, look for a subject by asking "who or what?" If you find a subject, <u>underline</u> it.
If there is no subject, mark Ph for phrase, and you're finished with that one.

Step 3)   If you have a verb and a subject, mark C for clause.

Check your answers on page 241.

EXAMPLE: The smallest turtle in the U.S.		Ph – C
1.	The bog turtle is the size of your palm	Ph – C
2.	Lives in the soggy soil of wetlands	Ph – C
3.	The Alabama beach mouse	Ph – C
4.	Makes its home in grassy sand dunes	Ph – C
5.	Construction threatens its habitat	Ph – C
6.	Snow monkeys are native to Japan	Ph – C
7.	Live farther north than any other monkey	Ph – C
8.	Thick, soft fur for warmth	Ph – C
9.	Snow monkeys bathe in the steaming water	Ph – C
10.	Of Japan's natural hot springs	Ph – C

Prepositional Phrases

Any group of words that doesn't have a subject and a verb is a phrase. Traditional grammar has names for many different kinds of phrases, but for correct writing and punctuation, the kind of phrase doesn't matter.

However, it is useful to know **prepositional phrases.**

A **preposition** is a word that tells what a cat can do with a chair.

A cat can be	**in** the chair
	under the chair
	beside the chair
	near the chair
	by the chair
	with the chair
A cat can jump	**over** the chair
	on the chair
	into the chair
	off the chair
	from the chair
A cat can run	**around** the chair
	to the chair
	through the legs of the chair
A cat can be so still that it looks like part	**of** the chair

Other prepositions include **about, along, at, beyond, beneath, between, for, like,** and more.

A **prepositional phrase** is a group of words that starts with a preposition and then has a couple more words to complete the idea.

The subject or verb of a sentence will never be inside a prepositional phrase. So if you have a long sentence, you could first put parentheses around all the prepositional phrases. Then just look at the words left over to find the subject and verb.

> The <u>cat</u> <u>ran</u> (around the chair) and <u>jumped</u> (into my lap).

> The <u>mouse</u> <u>peeked</u> out (of his hole), <u>darted</u> (across the floor), and <u>disappeared</u> (under the couch.)

> The <u>man</u> <u>sat</u> (on the grass) (under a shady tree) (in Central Park) (on a beautiful day) (in mid-July) listening (to his iPod).

Exercise 2.2 Identifying Prepositional Phrases

Put parentheses around the prepositional phrases, then mark the verbs and the subjects. Remember that neither the verb nor the subject will be inside a prepositional phrase. Check your answers on page 241.

1. Josie got lost in the old building.

2. The chess club will meet tomorrow in the library.

3. Max opened the heavy door, walked down the hall, went into the Registrar's office, sat in a chair, and waited his turn.

4. The mouse dashed out of the cat's paws and escaped into the woods.

5. Carrie placed her Hannah Montana CD collection in the trunk in the attic where she kept mementos from her childhood.

6. The archeologist found two vases of pure silver beneath a heap of rubble.

7. Renee took some yogurt out of the refrigerator, checked the expiration date, and dropped the yogurt into the trash can.

8. When the phone in the classroom rang, the students sitting by the teacher's desk jumped in their seats.

9. The Lamborghini sped around the curves coming dangerously close to the edge of the cliff.

10. Rene Descartes, a mathematician with considerable talent, invented a branch of mathematics known as analytical geometry.

Getting tricky . . .

If you can't sleep nights because you have to know the names for all the different kinds of phrases in traditional grammar, turn to page 226.

Subordinating Conjunctions

Think of some words that begin with the prefix *sub*.

submarine   subway

These things go under. The submarine goes under the water; the subway goes under the street.

subservient   submissive

These words describe someone who is less powerful. A person who is subservient or submissive willingly obeys someone else.

The prefix *sub* means under, less powerful.

A **subordinating conjunction** is a word that goes at the beginning of a clause and makes the clause less powerful or dependent on another clause.

Common Subordinating Conjunctions

after	although	as	because
before	if	since	so that
that	though	till	until
unless	when	where	while

Independent and Dependent Clauses

As you know, a **clause** is any group of words that has a subject and a verb. There are two kinds of clauses—dependent and independent—and they have different sounds.

When you put a **subordinating conjunction** at the beginning of a clause, the clause will sound different.

> I ate dinner.
> After I ate dinner . . .

Say both of these clauses out loud and listen to how your voice sounds. When you say the first clause, the pitch of your voice goes down, and you sound like you're finished talking. The first clause expresses a complete idea.

When you say the second clause, the pitch of your voice goes up, and it sounds like you are going to continue speaking and tell what happened after you ate dinner. This clause does not express a complete idea. The listener is waiting for you to finish.

> After I ate dinner . . . what happened?

A **subordinating conjunction** is a word that goes at the beginning of a clause and makes the clause sound unfinished.

Mark subordinating conjunctions with a wavy underline.

A **dependent clause** is a clause that starts with a subordinating conjunction. It sounds unfinished and leaves the reader hanging. Mark dependent clauses **DC.**

An **independent clause** does not have a subordinating conjunction. It sounds complete. Mark independent clauses **IC.**

> After I ate dinner, I washed the dishes.
>   DC   IC

The first clause depends on the second clause to finish the idea.

Common Subordinating Conjunctions

after	although	as	because
before	if	since	so that
that	though	till	until
unless	when	where	while

Getting tricky . . .

See page 156 for information on False Subordinating Conjunctions.

Exercise 2.3 Identifying Phrases, Independent Clauses, and Dependent Clauses

Step 1) Change the time and listen for a verb. If you find a verb, <u>double underline</u> it.
If there is no verb, mark **Ph** for phrase, and you're finished with that one.

Step 2) If you have a verb, look for a subject. Remember that the subject will almost always come before the verb. If you find a subject, <u>underline</u> it.
If there is no subject, mark **Ph** for phrase, and you're finished with that one.

Step 3) If you have a verb and a subject, it is a clause. Now you must determine what kind of clause. Look for a subordinating conjunction; it would be the first word of the clause. If you find a subordinating conjunction, underline it with a wavy line.

Step 4) If the clause has a subordinating conjunction, mark **DC** for dependent clause. If there is no subordinating conjunction, mark **IC** for independent clause.

Check your answers on page 242.

EXAMPLE: I hate mosquitos   Ph – **IC** – DC

1.   Always bite me   Ph – IC – DC

2.   I try to kill them   Ph – IC – DC

3.   When I am outside   Ph – IC – DC

4.   Drive me crazy   Ph – IC – DC

5.   While I mow the grass   Ph – IC – DC

6.   I can't swat them   Ph – IC – DC

7.   Because I have to push the mower   Ph – IC – DC

8.   Before I go outside   Ph – IC – DC

9.   I put on bug repellent spray   Ph – IC – DC

10. To keep the mosquitos away   Ph – IC – DC

Exercise 2.4 Identifying Phrases, Independent Clauses, and Dependent Clauses

Step 1)   Change the time and listen for a verb.
If you find a verb, <u>double underline</u> it.
If there is no verb, mark **Ph** for phrase, and you're finished with that one.

Step 2)   If you have a verb, look for a subject. Remember that the subject will almost always come before the verb.
If you find a subject, <u>underline</u> it.
If there is no subject, mark **Ph** for phrase, and you're finished with that one.

Step 3)   If you have a verb and a subject, it is a clause.
Now you must determine what kind of clause.
Look for a subordinating conjunction; it would be the first word of the clause. If you find a subordinating conjunction, underline it with a <u>wavy line</u>.

Step 4)   If the clause has a subordinating conjunction, mark **DC** for dependent clause. If there is no subordinating conjunction, mark **IC** for independent clause.

Check your answers on page 243.

EXAMPLE: The <u>Aztecs</u> <u>lived</u> in Mexico   Ph – **IC** – DC

1. In the fifteenth and early sixteenth centuries   Ph – IC – DC

2. Since the Aztec society had a strict class structure   Ph – IC – DC

3. At the top level of society   Ph – IC – DC

4. The nobles were all related to the emperor   Ph – IC – DC

5. Although the nobles performed different jobs   Ph – IC – DC

6. Such as judge, priest, or soldier   Ph – IC – DC

7. Middle class people were called commoners   Ph – IC – DC

8. Worked as farmers, merchants, and craftsmen   Ph – IC – DC

9. Slaves performed the hardest labor   Ph – IC – DC

10. Since they were at the bottom of the social structure   Ph – IC – DC

Exercise 2.5 Practice Identifying Phrases, Independent Clauses, and Dependent Clauses

Step 1) Change the tense and listen for a verb. If you find a verb, <u>double</u> <u>underline</u> it.
If there is no verb, mark **Ph** for phrase, and you're finished with that one.

Step 2) If you have a verb, look for a subject. Look for the subject in front of the verb. If you find a subject, <u>underline</u> it.
If there is no subject, mark **Ph** for phrase, and you're finished with that one.

Step 3) If you have a verb and a subject, it is a clause. Now you must determine what kind of clause.
Look for a subordinating conjunction; it would be the first word of the clause. If you find one, underline it with a <u>wavy line</u>.

Step 4) If the clause has a subordinating conjunction, mark **DC** for dependent clause. If there is no subordinating conjunction, mark **IC** for independent clause.

Check your answers on page 243.

EXAMPLE: Cell <u>phones</u> <u>are</u> everywhere   Ph – **IC** – DC

  1.   The new phone was too complicated   Ph – IC – DC

  2.   For Johnna's mom to use   Ph – IC – DC

  3.   She gave the phone to Johnna   Ph – IC – DC

  4.   When the phone bill came   Ph – IC – DC

5. The bill was extremely high   Ph – IC – DC

6. Because Johnna sent too many texts   Ph – IC – DC

7. On the bus, during lunch, and even   Ph – IC – DC
    in class

8. To pay her mom back   Ph – IC – DC

9. Johnna found a job   Ph – IC – DC

10. At the cell phone kiosk in the mall   Ph – IC – DC

The Sneaky, Mysterious, Invisible THAT

The word *that* can do many different jobs. It can be the subject of a sentence, or it can come at the end of a sentence.

> *That* is my car. I want to try *that*.

That can also be a subordinating conjunction. When *that* is functioning as a subordinating conjunction, is usually makes the second clause of a sentence dependent.

> I know that you ate my cookies!
> IC   DC

The word *that* has a tendency to go invisible.

> I know you ate my cookies!

We cannot see the word *that* in this sentence, but the meaning is still there. The second clause is still a dependent clause.

<u>I</u> <u><u>know</u></u> <u>you</u> <u><u>ate</u></u> my cookies!
   IC   DC

Pay attention when you speak, and you'll notice that we use the *invisible that* all the time.

Exercise 2.6 Identifying the Invisible *That*

<u>Double underline</u> the verbs and <u>underline</u> the subjects.

Write the word *that* under the sentence in the spot where it is invisible. One sentence has two dependent clauses and uses the invisible *that* two times. Check your answers on page 243.

EXAMPLE: <u>Gwendolyn</u> <u><u>knew</u></u> <u>Xavier</u> <u><u>loved</u></u> her.
                      <u>that</u>

1. For Valentine's day, Xavier knew Gwendolyn wanted roses.

2. But he was so broke he gave her freshly picked dandelions instead.

3. Gwendolyn was so disappointed she began to cry.

4. Xavier thought they were tears of joy she shed.

5. Gwendolyn wished Xavier would be a little more romantic.

Chapter Three

Fragments, Comma Splices, and Run-Ons

Fragments, comma splices, and run-ons are the most common mistakes that people make in their writing. In this chapter you will learn how to identify these mistakes and then how to fix them.

Sentence Fragments

A sentence must have an independent clause. A sentence that doesn't have an independent clause is called a **fragment**.

Remember:
An **independent clause** has a subject and a verb, and it expresses a complete idea.

<u>Mario</u> <u>hit</u> the winning run.   IC
The <u>weather</u> <u>was</u> cold.   IC

A **dependent clause** also has a subject and a verb, but it leaves the reader hanging. A dependent clause begins with a **subordinating conjunction** that changes the sound of the clause.

> <u>After</u> <u>Mario</u> <u>hit</u> the winning run . . . what?   DC
> <u>Although</u> the <u>weather</u> <u>was</u> cold . . . what?   DC

A **phrase** is any group of words that does not have a subject and a verb.

> in the morning   Ph
> wore a blue suit   Ph

Phrases and dependent clauses are important to our writing. They add details and make a sentence more interesting. But they cannot be sentences by themselves.

You will often see fragments in magazines, on billboards, and on your cereal box. If you are doing informal writing, go ahead and use fragments. For academic or business writing, it is better to write complete sentences.

Process for Identifying Fragments

Step 1)   Change the time and listen for a verb.
If you find a verb, <u>double underline</u> it and go on to the next step.
If there is no verb, the sentence is a phrase. Mark **F** for fragment.

Early in the morning.   **F**
After Mark <u>drove</u> all night.
(Go to the next step)

Step 2)   Next, look for a subject by asking "who?" If you find a subject, <u>underline</u> it and go on to the next step.
If there is no subject, the sentence is a phrase. Mark **F** for fragment.

<u>Drove</u> all night.   **F**
After <u>Mark</u> <u>drove</u> all night.
(Go to the next step.)

Step 3)   If you have a verb and a subject, it is a clause.
Now you must determine what kind of clause. Look for a subordinating conjunction. If you find one, underline it with a <u>wavy line</u>.
If the clause has a subordinating conjunction, it is a dependent clause. Mark **F** for fragment.

<u>After</u> <u>Mark</u> <u>drove</u> all night.   **F**

Step 4)   If the clause does not have a subordinating conjunction, it is an independent clause. Mark **OK** for a correct sentence.

<u>Mark</u> <u>drove</u> all night.   **OK**

Exercise 3.1 Identifying Fragments

Follow the steps: <u>Double underline</u> the verbs. <u>Underline</u> the subjects. Draw a <u>wavy line</u> under the subordinating conjunctions.

Mark phrases and dependent clauses **F**. Mark independent clauses **OK**. Check your answers on page 244.

EXAMPLE: The <u>capybara is</u> the world's largest rodent.   **OK**

1. Weighs more than one hundred pounds.   F – OK

2. Since its teeth grow continuously.   F – OK

3. The capybara chews on tough grasses.   F – OK

4. To keep its teeth short.   F – OK

5. They live near rivers, lakes, and swamps.   F – OK

6. In Central and South America.   F – OK

7. Capybaras are excellent swimmers.   F – OK

8. Because they have webbing between their toes. F – OK

9. When they are alarmed.   F – OK

10. They make a noise similar to a dog's bark.   F – OK

Exercise 3.2 Identifying Fragments

Step 1)   Change the time and listen for a verb. If you find a verb, <u>double underline</u> it. If there is no verb, the sentence is a phrase.

Mark **F** for fragment.

Step 2)   If you have a verb, look for a subject. If you find a subject, <u>underline</u> it. If there is no subject, the sentence is a phrase.

Mark **F** for fragment.

Step 3)   If you have a verb and a subject, it is a clause. Now you must determine what kind of clause. Look for a subordinating conjunction. If you find one, underline it with a <u>wavy line</u>.
If you have a subordinating conjunction, the clause is dependent.

Mark **F** for fragment.

Step 4)   If there is no subordinating conjunction, the clause is independent.

Mark **OK** for correct sentence.

Check your answers on page 244.

EXAMPLE: Over 2,200 earthworm <u>species</u> <u>exist</u>.   F – **OK**

1.   Earthworms live in all parts of the world.   F – OK

2.   Except in the Arctic and extremely arid regions.   F – OK

3. Although worms in the tropics grow up to   F – OK
    ten or eleven feet long.

4. Most earthworms are shorter.   F – OK

5. Usually one to two inches in length.   F – OK

6. An earthworm is typically gray or reddish   F – OK
    brown in color.

7. Five tiny hearts pump the worm's blood.   F – OK

8. Because earthworms are responsible for   F – OK
    aerating and mixing the soil.

9. Earthworms are vital to agriculture.   F – OK

10. As Charles Darwin discovered after he   F – OK
    studied them.

Exercise 3.3 Identifying Fragments

Step 1) Double underline the verbs. If there is no verb, the sentence is a phrase.

Mark **F** for fragment.

Step 2) Underline the subjects. If there is no subject, the sentence is a phrase.

Mark **F** for fragment.

Step 3) Underline subordinating conjunctions with a wavy line.

Mark the dependent clauses **F** for fragment.

Step 4) Mark the independent clauses **OK**.

Check your answers on page 244.

1. The 1960's marked the beginning of Rock and Roll.   F – OK

2. When the Beatles came to America In 1964.   F – OK

3. Next, the Rolling Stones arrived.   F – OK

4. Mick Jagger was the lead singer.   F – OK

5. In February of 1965.   F – OK

6. The Who made the charts in the U.K.   F – OK

7. After they recorded the hit song "I Can't Explain."   F – OK

8. In 1966 the Animals' "See See Rider" became a big hit in the U.S.   F – OK

9. In the late sixties.   F – OK

10. John Lennon left his wife for Yoko Ono.   F – OK

Fixing Fragments

There are two ways to fix a fragment, and they both involve erasing something.

First Method: You can erase a period and attach the fragment to a sentence that has an independent clause.

In the morning. <u>Sherry jogs</u> three miles.
Ph-fragment   IC

Erase the period to attach the fragment to a complete sentence:

> In the morning <u>Sherry</u> <u>jogs</u> three miles.
>   Ph   IC

By joining the fragment to a complete sentence, you created one longer sentence. One independent clause is enough even for a very long sentence.

Here's another example:

> <u>She</u> <u>goes</u> to the gym. <u>After</u> <u>she</u> <u>finishes</u> work.
>   IC   DC-fragment

Erase the period to attach the fragment to the complete sentence:

> <u>She</u> <u>goes</u> to the gym <u>after</u> <u>she</u> <u>finishes</u> work.
>   IC   DC

By joining the fragment and a complete sentence, you created one longer sentence.

Second method: If the fragment is a dependent clause, you can erase the subordinating conjunction and turn the dependent clause into an independent clause.

> <u>When</u> the <u>dog</u> <u>chews</u> the newspaper.
>   DC-fragment

Erase the subordinating conjunction:

The <u>dog</u> <u>chews</u> the newspaper.
　　　　IC

Now the sentence has an independent clause, so it is correct.

Here's another example:

<u>After</u> the <u>dog</u> <u>dug</u> up the flower bed.
　　　　　DC-fragment

Erase the subordinating conjunction:

The <u>dog</u> <u>dug</u> up the flower bed.
　　　　IC

Now the sentence has an independent clause, so it is correct.

Common Subordinating Conjunctions

after	although	as	because
before	if	since	so that
that	though	till	until
unless	when	where	while

Exercise 3.4 Fixing Fragments

Follow the steps: <u>Double underline</u> the verbs. <u>Underline</u> the subjects. Draw a <u>wavy line</u> under the subordinating conjunctions.

Any sentence that does not have an independent clause is a fragment. Fix the fragments by crossing out a period or by crossing out a subordinating conjunction.

Check your answers on page 245.

1. <u>Alex</u>, an African gray parrot, <u>was</u> thirty-one when he died. For thirty out of his thirty-one years <u>he</u> <u>lived</u> in a research lab. At Brandeis University.

2. Scientist Irene Pepperberg taught him to speak. Pepperberg believed. That animals had higher-order thinking capabilities.

3. When Pepperberg showed him two objects such as a green key and a green cup. Alex could identify the similarity by saying "color." To show the difference between the two items. He spoke the word "shape."

4. Alex also counted and did simple arithmetic. When Alex died in 2007. He had finally mastered saying the number seven.

5. Alex's accomplishments seem incredible. Because a parrot's brain is approximately the size of a walnut. Irene Pepperberg demonstrated that animals are capable of higher-level thinking.

Exercise 3.5 Fixing Fragments

Step 1) Change the tense and listen for a verb. If you find a verb, <u>double underline</u> it.

Step 2) If you have a verb, look for a subject. If you find a subject, <u>underline</u> it.

Step 3) If you have a verb and a subject, look for a subordinating conjunction at the beginning of the clause. If you find one, underline it with a wavy line.

Step 4) Any sentence that does not have an independent clause is a fragment. Fix the fragments by crossing out a period or by crossing out a subordinating conjunction.

Check your answers on page 245.

1. Gold has always fascinated humans. Because it is beautiful. As early as 3000 B.C.E., gold crafters in Mesopotamia Used gold to create jewelry.

2. Gold is a soft metal. Usually combined with other metals. Including copper or silver. Throughout history, only about 160,000 tons of gold have been mined. Enough to fill two Olympic-sized swimming pools.

3. Isaac Newton, once England's Master of the Mint, first created a standard price for gold. Although most countries stopped tying their currency to the gold standard long ago. The United States maintained its gold standard until 1971.

4. Gold is usually found with other metals. Such as mercury. After burning off the mercury. Miners sell the pure gold. When miners find gold mixed with copper. They ship it overseas to smelters. For separating the gold from the copper.

5. Although humans still want gold. Finding and mining new gold has become more difficult. Costing more and causing more damage to the environment.

Comma Splices and Run-Ons

Unlike fragments, which don't have an independent clause, a **comma splice** and a **run-on** both have two independent clauses.

The only difference between a comma splice and a run-on is that a comma splice has a comma between the two independent clauses and a run-on does not have a comma.

Mark comma splices **CS** and run-ons **RO**.

> Sue <u>cooked</u> dinner, <u>Joe</u> <u>washed</u> the dishes.   **CS**
>   IC   IC
>
> Sue <u>cooked</u> dinner <u>Joe</u> <u>washed</u> the dishes.   **RO**
>   IC   IC

Getting tricky . . .

Some people use the term **fused sentence** or **run-together** for a run-on.

Four Methods for Fixing Comma Splices and Run-Ons

Comma splices and run-ons are easy to fix. Instead of erasing something as you did to fix fragments, you add something. There are four different things you can add to fix comma splices or run-ons.

First Method: Add a **period** at the spot where the two clauses meet to separate the two clauses into two sentences.

> Sue cooked dinner, Joe washed the dishes.   **CS**
> <u>IC</u>   <u>IC</u>

> Sue cooked dinner. Joe washed the dishes.   **OK**
> <u>IC</u>   <u>IC</u>

Second Method: Add a comma and a **coordinating conjunction** between the two independent clauses.

Coordinating Conjunctions

For   And   Nor   But   Or   Yet   So

The seven **coordinating conjunctions** are very special words. They are all short words—only two or three letters long. They are the ONLY words that can be used with a comma to separate two independent clauses.

You can use the acronym FANBOYS to remember them.

> Sue cooked dinner, *and* Joe washed the dishes.   **OK**
> <u>IC</u>   <u>IC</u>

> Sue cooked dinner, *so* Joe washed the dishes.   **OK**
> <u>IC</u>   <u>IC</u>

Coordinating conjunctions are the ONLY words that can be used with a comma to separate two independent clauses. A comma with any other word gives you a comma splice.

> Sue cooked dinner, *therefore* Joe washed the dishes.   **CS**

Getting tricky . . .

SUB vs. CO

When we first learned about **subordinating conjunctions**, we looked at some words that begin with the prefix **sub**: submarine, subway, submissive.

We saw how the prefix **sub** means below or less powerful. A subordinating conjunction makes a clause less powerful—dependent—because the clause sounds unfinished.

After <u>we</u> <u>watched</u> the movie . . . . what happened?

Now think of some words that begin with the prefix **co**: cooperate, coworker, coexist.

The prefix **co** means together or equal. When you cooperate with someone, you work together. Your coworker is not your boss or your employee; you are equals. This is a very different meaning than sub.

A **coordinating conjunction** joins things that are equal, such as two independent clauses.

Third Method: You can add a **subordinating conjunction** at the beginning of one of the clauses to make the clause dependent. A comma splice or run-on occurs when you have two independent clauses. Make one of the clauses dependent, and you have solved the problem. Use whichever subordinating conjunction suits the meaning of your sentence.

Sue <u>cooked</u> dinner, <u>Joe</u> <u>washed</u> the dishes.   **CS**
IC   IC

<u>After</u> <u>Sue</u> <u>cooked</u> dinner, <u>Joe</u> <u>washed</u> the dishes.   **OK**
DC   IC

Sue <u>cooked</u> dinner <u>before</u> <u>Joe</u> <u>washed</u> the dishes.   **OK**
IC   DC

Notice that in the first sentence the dependent clause comes first and a comma follows it.

In the second sentence, the independent clause comes first, and there is no comma. That is the correct way to punctuate this type of sentence.

For more info on commas, turn to page 62.

Common Subordinating Conjunctions

after	although	as	because
before	if	since	so that
that	though	till	until
unless	when	where	while

Fourth Method: You can add a **semi-colon (;)** between the two clauses.

A semi-colon looks like exactly what it is. It is a half-way between a period and a comma. A semi-colon is big enough to separate the two independent clauses, but it is small enough that the two clauses are still one sentence.

<u>Sue</u> <u>cooked</u> dinner; <u>Joe</u> <u>washed</u> the dishes.   **OK**
  IC   IC

For a variation on the semi-colon method, you can also add a **conjunctive adverb** and a comma. Use whichever word suits the meaning of the sentence.

Common Conjunctive Adverbs

however	therefore
consequently	furthermore
nevertheless	hence
accordingly	moreover

<u>Sue</u> <u>cooked</u> dinner; *therefore,* <u>Joe</u> <u>washed</u> the dishes.
  IC   IC

<u>Sue</u> <u>cooked</u> dinner; *consequently,* <u>Joe</u> <u>washed</u> the dishes.
  IC   IC

Look carefully at the punctuation of these sentences. Put a semi-colon after the first independent clause. Then write the conjunctive adverb followed by a comma. Finally write the second independent clause.

> ## Getting tricky . . .
>
> The word **however** and the word **but** have essentially the same meaning. But when it comes to punctuation, they are totally different. **But** is a **coordinating conjunction**, one of those seven special little words that can be used with a comma to separate two independent clauses.
>
> **However** is a **conjunctive adverb**. Conjunctive adverbs can't do anything in your sentence except sound impressive. Unlike coordinating conjunctions, they can't join independent clauses, and unlike subordinating conjunctions, they don't make a clause dependent. They are purely decorative. If you want to put a conjunctive adverb between two independent clauses, go ahead, but be sure that you also use a semi-colon to separate the two clauses.

Exercise 3.6 Fixing Comma Splices and Run-ons

Double underline the verbs and underline the subjects. Then fix each comma splice or run-on using one of the methods indicated.

A. semi-colon alone
   Dogs bark; cats meow.

B. semi-colon with a conjunctive adverb and comma
   Dogs bark; however, cats meow.

C. comma with a coordinating conjunction
   <u>Dogs</u> <u>bark</u>, and <u>cats</u> <u>meow</u>.

D. period
   <u>Dogs</u> <u>bark</u>. <u>Cats</u> <u>meow</u>.

E. subordinating conjunction on the first clause
   <u>Although</u> <u>dogs</u> <u>bark</u>, <u>cats</u> <u>meow</u>.

F. subordinating conjunction on the second clause
   <u>Dogs</u> <u>bark</u> <u>while</u> <u>cats</u> <u>meow</u>.

Check your answers on page 246.

EXAMPLE:

                        , but
<u>Dinosaurs</u> <u>lived</u> long ago <u>they</u> <u>are</u> extinct now.   (C)

1. Dinosaurs are classified as reptiles they were cold blooded.   (F or A)

2. Carnivorous dinosaurs typically had pointy teeth an herbivore's teeth were flat.   (E or C)

3. Dinosaurs laid eggs most mothers abandoned their nests.   (B or C)

4. Recently discovered dinosaurs include many with unusual features scientists are trying to figure out the purpose of those features.   (D or A)

5. Digging up dinosaur bones is only the beginning for paleontologists the real challenge is assembling the skeleton.   (A or F or D)

Exercise 3.7 Fixing Comma Splices and Run-ons

<u>Double</u> <u>underline</u> the verbs and <u>underline</u> the subjects. Then fix each comma splice or run-on using one of the methods indicated.

    A. semi-colon alone

    B. semi-colon with a conjunctive adverb and comma

    C. comma with a coordinating conjunction

    D. period

    E. subordinating conjunction on the first clause

    F. subordinating conjunction on the second clause

Check your answers on page 247.

EXAMPLE:

<u>Benjamin Franklin</u> <u>was</u> a great man; <u>he</u> <u>lived</u> in Philadelphia.
(A)

1.   Franklin was born in 1706, he had sixteen brothers and sisters.   (A or C)

2.   Franklin wanted to be a writer he worked in his brother's printing shop.   (C or E)

3.   He was born in Boston Franklin moved to Philadelphia.   (C or E)

4.   In Philadelphia Franklin met and fell in love with Deborah, they got married.   (B or D)

5. He started a newspaper it was called *The Pennsylvania Gazette*. (A or C)

6. The paper was successful, Franklin became famous. (E or B)

7. Franklin was also an inventor, he invented the wood stove. (A or C)

8. He discovered that lightning is electricity he invented the lightning rod. (B or C)

9. Franklin traveled to England, he advocated for better treatment of the American colonies. (A or F)

10. Later he signed the Declaration of Independence he also signed the U.S. Constitution. (A or D)

Common Subordinating Conjunctions

after	although	as	because
before	if	since	so that
that	though	till	until
unless	when	where	while

Coordinating Conjunctions

For   And   Nor   But   Or   Yet   So

Common Conjunctive Adverbs

however	therefore
consequently	furthermore
nevertheless	hence
accordingly	moreover

Chapter Four

Commas

Commas can be tricky because we use them all the time to do many different jobs. One sentence may have three or more commas each doing a different job.

In this chapter you will first learn how to use basic commas—the four comma jobs that we use most often. These commas are not too difficult, and they account for probably ninety percent of the commas you need for your writing.

The second part of the chapter covers advanced commas which are more complicated, but fortunately we don't need them as often.

Basic Commas

The first four comma jobs are the ones you will use most often in your writing, and they are easy to learn.

Comma Job #1

Commas separate items in a list of three or more things:

> I like candy, pie, and cake.

The items in the list might be one word each or they might be more than one word:

> I like chocolate candy, apple pie, and carrot cake.

> I like eating chocolate candy, baking apple pies, and decorating cakes.

If you have more than three items in a list, put commas between all of them:

> I like candy, pie, cake, brownies, and ice cream.

If you have only two items in a list, don't put a comma:

> I hate spinach and liver.

Getting tricky . . .

Grammar books disagree about whether you should put a comma before the word **and** in a list. Some books say that the word **and** replaces the comma. Others say it is best to put the comma before the word **and**.

In this book you will see a comma before the word **and** in a list, but either style is correct.

If you're writing for school or business, ask your teacher or supervisor which style he or she prefers. For personal writing, use whichever style you prefer, but use it consistently.

Comma Job #2

Use a comma with a coordinating conjunction to join two independent clauses:

I <u>hate</u> cleaning the bathroom, *but* I <u>do</u> it every week.
  IC   IC

<u>Mike</u> <u>plays</u> first base, *and* <u>Devon</u> <u>plays</u> center field.
  IC   IC

Coordinating Conjunctions

For   And   Nor   But   Or   Yet   So

See page 49 for more about coordinating conjunctions joining independent clauses.

Comma Job #3

Use a comma to separate the parts of dates and place names:

> Caroline was born on July 25, 1995.
> Caroline was born in Tacoma, Washington.

If the sentence continues after the year or the state, put another comma after the year or the state.

> Caroline was born on July 25, 1995, on a Tuesday.

> Caroline was born in Tacoma, Washington, at Tacoma General Hospital.

Comma Job #4

Use a comma after **introductory material** such as a phrase or a dependent clause that appears at the beginning of a sentence.

> <u>Since</u> <u>he</u> <u>wants</u> to stay fit, <u>Mark</u> <u>exercises</u> every day.
>   DC   IC

> In order to stay fit, <u>Mark</u> <u>exercises</u> every day.
>   Ph   IC

Always use a comma after an **introductory dependent clause**. With an **introductory phrase**, a comma is needed only if the phrase is more than four words long. For a shorter phrase, use a comma only if it is needed for clarity.

But always use a comma after the name of a person spoken to or after the word **yes, no**, or **well** at the beginning of a sentence:

> Floyd, please close your mouth when you chew.
> Well, why don't you take your elbows off the table?

Exercise 4.1 Basic Commas

<u>Double underline</u> the verbs, <u>underline</u> the subjects, and draw a <u>wavy line</u> under the subordinating conjunctions.

Think about what is going on in each sentence and which comma job applies. Add commas where they are needed and write the number of the comma job at the end of each sentence. If you don't know what job the comma is doing, don't put a comma in that sentence.

> Job #1 – list of three or more things
> Job #2 – independent clauses with a coordinating
> conjunction
> Job #3 – dates and places
> Job #4 – introductory material

Some sentences will need several commas, and others won't need any.

Check your answers on page 248.

EXAMPLE:

On July 16, 2008, twelve <u>friends</u> <u>went</u> camping in the Northwest.
Job #3

1. First we unloaded all the gear from our cars and then we set up our tents and gathered firewood.

2. Since we didn't have a shower we washed in the river.

3. For dinner we caught some catfish in the river and fried them over the fire.

4. Fireflies crickets and frogs entertained us as we sat around a campfire and swatted the mosquitoes away.

5. We unpacked the marshmallows chocolate bars and graham crackers and made smores.

6. After our hands and mouths were thoroughly sticky people began to head toward their tents to sleep.

7. Everyone was bedded down and sleeping soundly when rain began to fall.

8. One minute the rain fell in a drizzle and the next minute we were caught in a torrential downpour.

9. After the wind knocked one tent over everyone started to reconsider the wisdom of camping.

10. Around 2 a.m. we decided to pack up our tents and drive to Missoula Montana to stay in the Motel 6.

Exercise 4.2 Basic Commas

<u>Double underline</u> the verbs, <u>underline</u> the subjects, and draw a <u>wavy line</u> under the subordinating conjunctions.

Think about what is going on in each sentence and which comma job applies. Add commas where they are needed, and write the number of the comma job at the end of each sentence. If you don't know what job the comma is doing, don't put a comma in that sentence.

> Job #1 – list of three or more things
> Job #2 – independent clauses with a coordinating
> conjunction
> Job #3 – dates and places
> Job #4 – introductory material

Some sentences will need several commas, and others won't need any.

Check your answers on page 249.

EXAMPLE:

<u>Gerbils</u> <u>are</u> hard to catch <u>because</u> <u>they</u> <u>are</u> little, fast, and slippery.
Job #1

1. On May 15 2012 we came home from the grocery store to find that our pet gerbil had escaped from his cage.

2. Leo had chewed a hole in his cage so we closed the front door to keep him from running outside.

3. Since we couldn't open the door we passed the grocery bags in through an open window.

4. As soon as we put the groceries away we started looking for Leo.

5. We looked under the couch behind the dresser and even in the bathtub.

6. We even looked under all the dirty clothes on my brother's bedroom floor.

7. We didn't find Leo but we found three quarters a marble and a stale granola bar.

8. After several hours of searching we gave up.

9. Before going to sleep we rigged up a gerbil trap and filled it with sunflower seeds.

10. We woke up on May 16 2012 to find Leo sleeping in the trap and that same day we bought him a stronger cage.

Advanced Commas

There are only three more comma jobs. These three are somewhat tricky, but you won't need them too often in your writing.

Comma Job #5

Use one or two commas to separate a **conjunctive adverb** from the sentence. Conjunctive adverbs are impressive-sounding words that show the relationship between ideas.

Common Conjunctive Adverbs

however	therefore
consequently	furthermore
nevertheless	hence
accordingly	moreover

First we will look at conjunctive adverbs in a sentence with just one clause.

If the conjunctive adverb comes at the beginning or end of the sentence, separate it with one comma. If the conjunctive adverb comes in the middle of the clause, separate it with a comma before and a comma after.

> *Consequently,* Miss America will relinquish her crown effective immediately.

> The Miss America crown, *therefore,* will go to the first runner up.

> The former Miss America will keep her bouquet of roses, *however.*

Conjunctive adverbs can also be used between two independent clauses. In this case, use a semi-colon before the conjunctive adverb and a comma after.

> The temperature was 105 degrees; *consequently,* we postponed the hike.

> I want to go to the party; *however,* I have to finish my homework first.

If you're having a déjà vu experience, it's because you already learned this on page 52.

Comma Job #6

Use a comma to separate **coordinate adjectives**.

An **adjective** is a word that modifies or describes a noun. **Coordinate** means equal. Adjectives are common, but it is rare for them to be coordinate.

> The dog had tangled dirty fur.

In this sentence *tangled* and *dirty* are both adjectives describing the fur.

There are two tests you can use to determine if the adjectives are coordinate. The first test is to reverse the words:

> The dog had dirty tangled fur.

That sounds okay. The second test is to say the word *and* between the two adjectives:

> The dog had tangled and dirty fur.

That sounds okay. These two adjectives passed the tests. They are coordinate, so you should put a comma between them:

> The dog had tangled, dirty fur.

Here is another sentence.

> He wore a new blue suit.

Use the two tests to see if the adjectives *new* and *blue* are equal. First, reverse the words:

> He wore a blue new suit.

That sounds funny. Try the second test:

> He wore a new and blue suit.

That sounds funny too. These adjectives did not pass the tests. They are not coordinate, so don't put a comma between them:

> He wore a new blue suit.

What if the two adjectives pass one test but not the other? That hardly ever happens, but if it does, you can decide whether to put the comma or not. In the vast majority of cases, two adjectives will not be coordinate.

For more info on adjectives, see page 233.

Comma Job #7

Use commas to separate **non-essential material** from the sentence. **Non-essential** means extra, not necessary to the meaning of the sentence.

Kids *who watch TV all day* are lazy.

To determine whether you should put commas around the middle part of this sentence, you must decide if those words are extra. Would the meaning of the sentence change if you removed those middle words?

Kids are lazy.

This sentence does not have the same meaning as the original sentence. It sounds as if all kids are lazy, not just kids who watch TV all day. Since these words are not extra, you should not put commas around them:

Kids who watch TV all day are lazy.

Here is another one.

Jason *who watches TV all day* is lazy.

Here you see the same words in the middle of the sentence. What happens if you take them out this time?

Jason is lazy.

This sentence doesn't tell us why Jason is lazy, but the meaning is the same. In this case, those middle words are extra, or non-essential, so you should put commas around them:

Jason, who watches TV all day, is lazy.

One particular type of non-essential element is an **appositive**, a word or group of words that renames somebody or something. Sometimes an appositive is extra (non-essential) and sometimes it is needed.

My brother Louis teaches SCUBA diving.

The appositive here is *Louis.* I already named him once when I said *my brother.* When I give his first name, I am naming him again. That's an appositive.

Now I have to decide if *Louis* is extra or not. The real question is how many brothers do I have? If I have two brothers, the reader wouldn't know which brother I mean. His name would not be extra, so I would not put commas.

Here's my sentence if I have two brothers:

My brother Louis teaches SCUBA diving.

But if I have only one brother, there is only one person I could mean by *my brother.* In this case, the name *Louis* would be extra, so I would put commas around his name.

Here's my sentence if I have only one brother:

My brother, Louis, teaches SCUBA diving.

Your use of commas tells the reader whether you have one brother or more than one.

Be careful—When you're looking for non-essential elements, don't get carried away. Look at this sentence:

> Jennifer has a red car.

What word in the middle of this sentence could be left out? *Red*. But should you put commas around the word *red*? No.

Commas have a certain sound to them. They tell the reader to put a little pause or give a little emphasis. If you pause before and after the word *red*, the sentence will sound strange:

> Jennifer has a . . . *RED* . . . car.

When you're considering putting commas around something in the middle of a sentence, first make sure it really is extra, and then also think about whether you want the sound of commas there.

Exercise 4.3 Advanced Commas

Think about what is going on in each sentence and which comma job applies. Add commas where they are needed, and write the number of the comma job at the end of each sentence.

> Job #5 – conjunctive adverbs
> Job #6 – coordinate adjectives
> Job #7 – non-essential material

Common Conjunctive Adverbs

however	therefore
consequently	furthermore
nevertheless	hence
accordingly	moreover

Some sentences will need one comma, some will need two, and others won't need any.

Check your answers on page 249.

EXAMPLE: Monica brushed her long, shiny hair. *Job #6*

1. The noisy excited kids crowded into the movie theater.

2. That old blue car is good enough for driving to work.

3. My mother the lady in the pink suit is the keynote speaker.

4. People who live in glass houses shouldn't throw stones.

5. Football players therefore spend a great deal of time in the weight room.

6. Dogs that bark all night long drive me crazy.

7. Domesticated dogs which are descended from wolves are good family pets.

8. The landlord finally replaced the apartment's orange shag carpet.

9. The imitation paneling however will not be replaced until next year.

10. People who don't brush and floss have a much higher incidence of cavities.

This exercise was challenging. Commas can be tricky, so don't be discouraged if you had problems. Check your answers and try to understand any mistakes you made.

Exercise 4.4 Advanced Commas

Think about what is going on in each sentence and which comma job applies. Add commas where they are needed, and write the number of the comma job at the end of each sentence.

Job #5 – conjunctive adverbs
Job #6 – coordinate adjectives
Job #7 – non-essential material

Common Conjunctive Adverbs

however	therefore
consequently	furthermore
nevertheless	hence
accordingly	moreover

Some sentences will need one comma, some will need two or three, and others won't need any.

Check your answers on page 250.

EXAMPLE:

Monica brushed her long, shiny hair.   *Job #6*

1. The patient walked into the cold cramped waiting
   room.   *6*

2. Abraham Lincoln author of the Gettysburg Address is
   considered one of America's greatest orators.   *7*

3. San Francisco however has a much cooler climate
   than Los Angeles.   *5*

4. The barista squirted heavy whipping cream onto the
   steaming vanilla latte   *none*

5. During flu season we should all thank the person who
   invented the paper tissue.   *none*

6. The granite countertops a last minute addition sent
   the new house over budget.   *7*

7. Roberto scanned the bleachers of the school's gym for
   his girlfriend Jasmine and her friends.   *4*

8. Consequently the teacher suggested that Monica get
   an early start on writing her long complicated research paper.   *5 - 6*

9. The girl who brought a snake to school received two
   days of suspension.   *none*

10. The soft lights in the counselor's office however con-
    trasted with her loud bossy personality.
                                     5 - 6

Why Commas Drive People Crazy

So far we have only dealt with one comma job at a time. In real-life writing, it is quite common for a sentence to need several commas, each one doing a different job.

Most of the comma jobs are fairly easy. The challenging aspect of commas is figuring out what's going on in your sentence and which comma job applies.

Exercise 4.5 Analyzing Comma Jobs

In the sentences below, the commas are already in their correct places. Figure out which job each comma is doing and write the number of that job at the end of the sentence.

> Job #1 – list of three or more things
> Job #2 – two independent clauses with a coordinating
>   conjunction
> Job #3 – dates and places
> Job #4 – introductory material
> Job #5 – conjunctive adverb
> Job #6 – coordinate adjective
> Job #7 – non-essential material

Check your answers on page 251.

EXAMPLE: While Felix washed the cars, Pam cleaned the kitchen, living room, and bathrooms.   *Job # 4 & #1*

1.   Benjamin Franklin was born in Boston, Massachusetts, but he later moved to Philadelphia, Pennsylvania.

3, 2

2. Monkeys have tails, but gorillas do not have tails; they are both primates, however.

3. People who can't drive must take the bus, the train, or the subway.

4. While Gloria looked in the mirror, the hairdresser styled her long, beautiful hair.

5. Melissa's husband, Todd, likes to fish, hunt, and hike.

6. After hiking all day, Todd soaked his swollen, aching feet.

7. They met February 14, 2011, at a party, and they were married on February 14, 2012.

8. I had not planned to go out this evening; I could, however, be persuaded.

9. On the first day of kindergarten, Maria watched her eldest daughter, Katie, get on the school bus.

10. Daniel washed the car, mowed the grass, and trimmed the bushes; consequently, his muscles were sore that evening.

Chapter Five

Other Punctuation and Mechanics

This chapter covers all the other punctuation marks besides commas—apostrophes, dashes, colons, and semi-colons—as well as the rules for capitalization, punctuating dialogue, and writing out numbers.

Apostrophes

We use apostrophes in contractions and to show possession.

Apostrophe Job #1

Use an apostrophe to indicate where letters have been removed to form a contraction.

> I do not play chess.   I don't play chess.

Most contractions are easy, but some are tricky:

I would   I'd
I'd love to go to Hawaii for vacation.

I had   I'd
I'd already paid for my groceries when I remembered my coupons.

He would   he'd
He'd rather play golf than mow the lawn.

She had   she'd
She'd already lost four golf balls before she reached the second hole.

Let us   let's
Let's go out for dinner tonight.

You are   you're
You're not wearing that to the party, are you?
Use an apostrophe when you mean YOU ARE.

It is   it's
It's so hot today; let's go swimming.
Use an apostrophe when you mean IT IS.

They are   they're
They're saving up to buy a house.
Use an apostrophe when you mean THEY ARE.

When we're talking, we use contractions all the time. In writing, it is not wrong to use contractions, but they do make your writing sound rather informal. In a paper for school or a business letter, it's usually best to avoid contractions.

Getting tricky . . .

You're, it's, and **they're** are tricky because they have homophones: words that sound the same but have different spellings and different meanings. The chapter on homophones begins on page 137.

Apostrophe Job #2

Use **'s** to indicate possession.

Possession includes not only ownership of a material object but also relationships and ideas:

Material Possessions:
Billy's tricycle
Carrie's house
the library's books
the dog's bone

Relationships:
Ethan's mom
Linda's sister
the car's driver
the company's staff

Ideas and Non-Material Things:
Selma's responsibility
Bob's problem
Grace's concern
the cat's personality
the nation's economic outlook

When you start thinking about apostrophes, it is tempting to put an apostrophe in every word that ends with an **s**. If the **s** is just indicating plural, not possession, don't put an apostrophe.

> That is Adam's bike.
> > Does Adam own anything?
> > Yes. Adam owns a bike; use an apostrophe.

> Two cars were in the garage.
> > Do the cars own anything?
> > No, there is just more than one of them.
> > Don't use an apostrophe.

> Three mayors had a conference.
> > Do the mayors own anything?
> > No, there is just more than one of them.
> > Don't use an apostrophe.

> The cat's food bowl is empty.
> > Does the cat own anything?
> > Yes. The cat owns a bowl.
> > Use an apostrophe.

Possession with words ending in S

If a word ends with the letter **s**, you don't need to add another **s**. Just put an apostrophe at the end of the word to indicate possession.

Carlos owns a dog.	Carlos' dog
Dennis owns a stereo.	Dennis' stereo
Mr. Jones owns a car.	Mr. Jones' car

Sometimes the word ends with **s** because two people own something together. Imagine two dogs who share their dog house.

Two dogs own a house.	Dogs' house

Just as with the name *Carlos*, the word *dogs* ends with an **s**. You don't need to add another **s**; just add the apostrophe. But be careful to place the apostrophe at the end of the word: dogs'.

Actually, the placement of the apostrophe shows whether one or two or more dogs (or people) own something because the apostrophe marks the end of the word. Does the dog have his own house, or does he have to share?

My cat's ball	Look at the letters that come before the apostrophe: cat. That's one cat. She has her own ball.
The boys' bedroom	Look at the letters that come before the apostrophe: boys. That's more than one boy. Two (or more) boys are sharing.

Exercise 5.1 Apostrophes

Add apostrophes where they are needed. Some sentences need more than one apostrophe, and others don't need any. Check your answers on page 252.

1. The announcers voice echoed throughout the stadium.

2. The Beatles first appeared on Ed Sullivans variety show on August 24, 1964.

3. Jack Parr—Ed Sullivans main rival—had aired footage of the Beatles in January 1964.

4. The professors car was towed because it was parked in the students lot.

5. Sams cats favorite game is clawing the drapes.

6. The name Matthew means "Gods gift," while Samanthas meaning is "God heard us."

7. England has had six kings named George.

8. "Lets review for the test," announced the professors assistant.

9. Graphing calculators are essential for students in upper-level math classes.

10. Even though Frances owned a car, she had to borrow her roommates car for trips over five miles.

Exercise 5.2 Apostrophes

Add apostrophes where they are needed. Some sentences need more than one apostrophe, and others don't need any. Check your answers on page 253.

1. The author's previous lectures had been wildly successful.

2. Six hundred people purchased their tickets months in advance to reserve their spots.

3. Early in the morning, the auditorium's air conditioning units malfunctioned.

4. The program's producer called a repair crew.

5. When the repair techs arrived, they couldn't fix the air conditioners because they didn't have the right parts.

6. Sweat dripped down the author's face as she began the lecture.

7. Some paramedics arrived to treat a man who had fainted in the auditorium's stifling heat.

8. The author didn't want any lawsuits, so she stopped in the middle of the speech and asked the box office to refund the audience's money.

9. The people's impatience with the two employees trying to issue refunds created an even more unpleasant situation.

10. When they left, everyone had experienced the author's message—global warming.

Exercise 5.3 Plural Possessives

In the following sentences, look at the letters that come before the apostrophe. Then mark **one** or **more than one**.

Check your answers on page 254.

EXAMPLE:

The **dog**'s bowl is blue.

one dog
more than one

1. The cats' clawing pole is ragged.

one cat
more than one

2. The goose's honk was loud.

one goose
more than one

3. The student's work was correct.

one student
more than one

4. The women's restroom was crowded.

one woman
more than one

5. The birds' nest was on a branch.

one bird
more than one

6. The squirrel's nest was in a tree.

one squirrel
more than one

7. The children's playroom was messy.   one child
                                           more than one

8. The man's coat was warm.   one man
                                           more than one

Capitalization

Capitalization is one of the first things children learn in school. Most of the capitalization rules are very easy, but a few of them can cause problems for writers.

Capitalization Rule #1

Use a capital letter for people's names and titles that precede the name:

Mr. Smith	Rev. Jones
Miss Baxter	King Henry
Senator Brown	President Washington
Uncle Charley	Principal Jackson

Capitalization Rule #2

Use a capital letter for family titles when you could replace the title with the person's first name.

When Mom and Dad got home, Grandma said the kids had been very good.

In this sentence, the family titles are capitalized because it sounds fine to replace the family titles with the first names:

When Mary and Steve got home, Barbara said the kids had been very good.

Here is another sentence:

My Mary gave my Steve a sweater for his birthday.

This sounds funny. Don't capitalize the family titles in this sentence because you can't replace them with the names.

My mom gave my dad a sweater for his birthday.

Capitalization Rule #3

Use a capital letter for the days of the week, the months of the year, and for holidays:

Monday   April   Independence Day

Capitalization Rule #4

Capitalize the names of ethnic groups, nationalities, and languages:

African-American	Chinese
Spanish	Asian
British	Arabic
Latino	Polynesian
English	Caucasian
Australian	Greek

What about *black* and *white* when referring to race? Whether you capitalize these words depends on whom you're writing for. When writing for school, don't capitalize them unless your teacher tells you to. If you are writing for a publication that capitalizes these words as part of its official style, then follow that style.

Capitalization Rule #5

Capitalize the names of specific things, but don't capitalize general things.

Specific Things:	General Things:
Africa	continent
Pacific Ocean	ocean
Spain	country
Mount Kilimanjaro	mountain
Paris	city
Main Street	street
the Empire State Building	office building
S.S. Titanic	ship
Starship Enterprise	spaceship
Magic Shears Hair Salon	beauty parlor
Nikes	tennis shoes
Wheaties	cereal
President Washington	the president
Christianity	religion
Jewish	faith
Episcopal	church

Did you know?

Italicize (or underline) the title of a long work, such as a book, magazine, movie, or CD:

The Grapes of Wrath (book)
Sports Illustrated (magazine)
Titanic (movie)
Blues Train (CD)

Put quote marks around the titles of short works or works that appear inside a larger work such as an article in a magazine or newspaper, a song on a CD, etc.:

"Carter wins Nobel Prize" (magazine article)
"Fast Train" (song on a CD)

Capitalization Rule #6

Capitalize the first word and the important words in the title of a book, movie, etc.

Of Mice and Men
Better Homes and Gardens
Raiders of the Lost Ark

Exercise 5.4 Capitalization

Capitalize words as needed. Check your answers on page 254.

1. for christmas aunt josephine gave my mother a poodle named ruffles.

2. many american companies have factories in other countries; for example, some texas instruments calculators are made in utrecht, netherlands.

3. next monday school will end at 11:30 so that the teachers can meet with parents while superintendent toni godwin meets with the administrators.

4. vincent d'onofrio plays robert goren, one of TV's most fascinating detectives; his partner, alex eames, played by kathryn erbe, has been called the dr. watson to goren's sherlock holmes.

5. Many english words have spanish origins, including alligator, plaza, and stampede.

Exercise 5.5 Capitalization

Capitalize words as needed.

Check your answers on page 255.

EXAMPLE:

This year Christmas is on a Monday.

1. we will go to grandma's house for dinner.

2. my grandma makes great christmas cookies.

3. for thanksgiving mom always bakes pumpkin pie.

4. my dad loves thanksgiving because he likes to eat.

5. miss dixon went to tokyo on her vacation.

6. most of the people in israel are jewish.

7. on wednesdays i go to my spanish class.

8. columbus sailed to america with the nina, the pinta, and the santa maria.

9. many asian people live in san francisco.

10. we could go to an italian restaurant, a mexican restaurant, or a french restaurant.

Punctuating Dialogue

Dialogue is words spoken out loud.

1. Start a new paragraph each time a different person speaks.

2. Put quotation marks around the words spoken.

3. Begin the spoken words with a capital letter.

4. Place a period, question mark, exclamation point, comma, or semi-colon inside the quotation marks.

5. Separate the *he said/she said* from the words spoken with a comma (or question mark, etc.).

6. You can omit the *he said/she said* as long as the reader will be able to tell who is saying what.

The easiest way to learn how to punctuate dialogue is to follow the example of any novel.

> Maggie and Jackie were standing at the corner waiting for the bus. It was a cold November morning, and the wind was howling.
> "My fingers are freezing!" Maggie said.
> Jackie agreed, "Mine too, and my nose is like ice."
> "It seems like we've been waiting for twenty minutes," Maggie said.
> "I know. I wonder if the bus is late or if it's just because we're so cold," said Jackie.

"Do you have a watch on?" Maggie asked.

"No," answered Jackie, "but I'll look on my cell phone."

"Wait!" Maggie said, "here it comes now." They watched as the bus came around the corner.

"It's coming awfully fast," said Jackie. The bus hit a patch of ice and spun in a circle before coming to a stop.

For information about punctuating quotations in a research paper, turn to page 187.

Numbers

Spell numbers that can be expressed with one or two words:

one	thirty-three	two thousand
seventeen	one hundred	five million

If three or more words are needed to express a number, use numerals instead.

101	3, 015	7,429	5,000,003

But always spell out a number that is the first word of the sentence.

Nineteen sixty-four was a great year.
I was born in **1964**.

Hyphens and Dashes

A **hyphen** is used to join words:

sister-in-law	five-year-old
two-fifths	pre-2001
un-American	president-elect

A **dash** is used to separate parts of a sentence. Make a dash by typing two hyphens. Many computer programs will join the two hyphens together into one long dash.

A dash can be used in the same places you would use a comma, but a dash gives a longer pause and a greater sense of emphasis. Use a dash when you want a dramatic effect:

> I have had quite an exciting day—but you wouldn't want to hear about it, would you?

> Marcus said—brace yourself!—he has been accepted to Harvard!

> Her three best friends—Jill, Jan, and Joan—gave her a surprise birthday party.

Colons

Colons are more formal than dashes. A colon is used only after an independent clause; the first part of the sentence must be able to stand alone. The colon introduces a list or an example.

> Her essay contained numerous grammatical errors: comma splices, fragments, and misspellings, just to name a few.

> I have three favorite authors: Dickens, Steinbeck, and Austen.

> There was only one hope: we had to find an antidote.

Notice that in each of these sentences, the first part could stand alone. It is an independent clause with a complete idea:

> Her essay contained numerous grammatical errors.
> I have three favorite authors.
> There was only one hope.

For an explanation of independent clauses, turn to page 28.

Here are some sentences in which a colon is used incorrectly. See if you can tell what's wrong:

> Her essay contained numerous grammatical errors such as: comma splices, fragments, and misspellings.

> My three favorite authors are: Dickens, Steinbeck, and Austen.

> Our only hope was: we had to find an antidote.

Do you see what's wrong? The words before the colon do not express a complete idea by themselves:

> Her essay contained numerous grammatical errors such as.

> My three favorite authors are.

> Our only hope was.

In these sentences the words before the colon can not stand alone, so a colon is not appropriate. Actually, no punctuation is needed:

> Her essay contained numerous grammatical errors such as comma splices, fragments, and misspellings.

> My three favorite authors are Dickens, Steinbeck, and Austen.

> Our only hope was we had to find an antidote.

One other use for a colon is to set off the subtitle of a book. Many non-fiction books will have a title and a subtitle. The cover of the book looks like this:

A World Lit Only by Fire

The Medieval Mind and the Renaissance
by William Manchester

If you need to give the name of this book in a sentence, punctuate it like this:

I just finished reading *A World Lit Only by Fire: The Medieval Mind and the Renaissance* by William Manchester.

Even though the title is not italicized on the cover of the book, you should italicize (or underline) the title in your writing.

For info on italicizing or using quote marks around titles, see page 90.

Semi-Colons

A period and a comma met at a party. They fell in love, got married, and had a beautiful baby that was a semi-colon. A semi-colon is halfway between a period and a comma. It is smaller than a period but bigger than a comma.

Semi-colon Job #1

The most common use of a semi-colon is to separate two independent clauses as explained on page 52.

> <u>Jill</u> <u>wanted</u> Mexican food; <u>Jason</u> <u>wanted</u> pizza.
>   IC   IC

Semi-colon Job #2

Semi-colons are also used to separate items in a list when the items contain commas, such as place names:

> I've lived in Tallahassee, Florida; Tacoma, Washington; and Raleigh, North Carolina.

Normally items in a list would be separated by commas as explained on page 60. But in this case, using only commas would make the sentence confusing:

> I've lived in Tallahassee, Florida, Tacoma, Washington, and Raleigh, North Carolina.

This sentence reads like six places rather than three places with two names each. Semi-colons divide up the list more clearly.

Exercise 5.6 Colons, Dashes, and Semi-Colons

Add colons, dashes, and semi-colons where needed. Some sentences need more than one type of punctuation mark. One sentence does not need any additional punctuation.

Check your answers on page 255.

1. The most popular sports in America are football, basketball, and baseball.

2. America's most popular sports football, basketball, and baseball are viewed by millions every year.

3. As an executive assistant for marketing, Jaime has traveled to three major international cities this year Lima, Peru Sydney, Australia and Rome, Italy.

4. Hillside High's Brad Pitt no relation to the famous actor has three favorite teachers Mr. Smith, Mrs. Wilkins, and Ms. Cassidy.

5. The week before Christmas, the malls are packed with people buying gifts the week after Christmas, the malls are packed with people returning gifts.

6. My old car got twelve miles per gallon my new car gets thirty.

7. Stefan a true coffee snob will only drink Starbuck's espresso.

8. Only one thing kept me from flying to Acapulco for spring break I didn't have any money.

9. Jan spent her spring break in Acapulco she went to Aspen for Christmas.

10. When you're buying real estate, only three things matter location, location, and location.

Chapter Six

Case and Agreement

This chapter covers pronoun case, pronoun–antecedent agreement, and subject–verb agreement.

Pronouns

A **pronoun** is a word that replaces another word:

> Superman is faster than a speeding bullet.
> He is more powerful than a locomotive.
> He can leap tall buildings in a single bound.

He is the pronoun that replaces the word *Superman.*

Superman is the **antecedent** (ant-eh-SEE-dent). The prefix *ante* means before, so the antecedent is the word that comes before the pronoun. The antecedent is the word that the pronoun is replacing.

When you're writing, make sure that your reader can easily identify the antecedent for each pronoun.

> Sue, Sally, and Samantha went rollerblading.
> She fell and broke her wrist.

In the second sentence, the pronoun is *she*, but the antecedent is unclear. You can't tell which woman fell. This mistake is called **unclear pronoun reference** because it is unclear which antecedent the pronoun is referring to. In this type of sentence, use the person's name instead of a pronoun.

> Sue, Sally, and Samantha went rollerblading.
> Sally fell and broke her wrist.

For more information on pronouns and the nouns they replace, see page 229.

Did you know?

We use the prefix **ante** all the time: I woke up at 7 a.m.

The abbreviation a.m. stands for ante meridian. **Ante** means before, and **meridian** means middle of the day or noon.

The abbreviation p.m. stands for post meridian. **Post** means after.

Pronoun Case

Pronouns can be tricky because different forms of the pronoun need to be used for different functions in a sentence. This is called **pronoun case.**

If the pronoun is serving as the subject of the sentence, we use **subjective case:**

> *I* took my dog with me.

If the pronoun is showing ownership, we use **possessive case:**

> I took *my* dog with me.

If the pronoun comes at the end of a clause or phrase, we typically use **objective case:**

> I took my dog with *me.*

These three pronouns—*I, my, me*—all refer to the same person, but we need all three words because each pronoun is serving a different function. If you mix up the cases, the sentence will sound funny:

> Me took I dog with my.

If English is your first language, you automatically use the correct case for pronouns most of the time:

You took your dog with you.
He took his dog with him.
She took her dog with her.
We took our dog with us.
They took their dog with them.

You don't often hear people say:

Me washed the car.
Him washed the car.
You can ride to the game with I.
You can ride to the game with he.

But when a sentence has two names together, choosing the correct case is not so easy. You may often hear people make mistakes:

Me and Mike washed the car.
Mike and him washed the car.

You can ride to the game with Joe and I.
You can ride to the game with he and Joe.

Choosing the Correct Case

To choose the correct pronoun case in a sentence that has another name, leave out the name, and you will know which pronoun sounds right:

Sheila went shopping with Rachel and (I or me?)

Leave out Rachel's name to see what sounds right.

> Sheila went shopping with I.

That doesn't sound right.

> Sheila went shopping with me.

Yes, that's right. Now put Rachel's name back in:

> Sheila went shopping with Rachel and me.

Here's another one:

> (He or him?) and Joel won the tennis championship.

Leave out Joel's name to see what sounds right.

> Him won the tennis championship.

That doesn't sound right.

> He won the tennis championship.

Yes, that's right. Now put Joel's name back in:

> He and Joel won the tennis championship.

Use the same process if the sentence has two pronouns:

> (Her or she?) and (I or me?) decorated the room.

Leave out the second set of pronouns to see which word sounds right in the first set.

> Her decorated the room.

That doesn't sound right.

> She decorated the room.

That's right. Now you can choose the second pronoun by leaving out the first one:

> Me decorated the room.

That doesn't sound right.

> I decorated the room.

That's right. Now put them both together:

> She and I decorated the room.

Exercise 6.1 Pronoun Case

Circle the correct pronoun. Check your answers on page 256.

1. The first-place prize in the school's robot contest went to Eric and (I – me).

2. Cecilia and (I – me) took turns driving home for Spring Break.

3. Mark invited (I – me) to play golf with (he – him) and Julian.

4. (She – Her) and Patty spent all day stripping wallpaper.

5. Be sure to call (we – us) as soon as you hear from (they – them).

6. (Him – He) and (her – she) have decided to go to Hawaii for their honeymoon.

7. I know (him – he) and (her – she) will have a wonderful trip.

8. Martha is coming over this afternoon to help Emily and (I – me) clean out the attic.

9. Nothing could have prepared (they – them) for the surprise when (they – them) won the lottery.

10. On Thanksgiving, (we – us) all go to Grandma's house to eat the wonderful meal (her – she) and Grandpa have prepared.

Pronoun Agreement

What's wrong with this sentence?

John went rock climbing, and she pulled a muscle.

John is a man and doesn't want to be called *she.*

John went rock climbing, and they pulled a muscle.

John is one person, and the word *they* makes him sound like more than one.

A pronoun needs to **agree with** or match its antecedent. It needs to agree in terms of gender (John is a man; don't call him *she*), and it needs to agree in terms of number (John is one person; don't call him *they*).

Usually we choose the correct pronoun easily. But in certain tricky sentences, people often make a mistake.

Singular Indefinite Pronouns

everyone	someone	anyone	no one
everybody	somebody	anybody	nobody
each	either	neither	

These pronouns are called indefinite because they don't refer to a specific person. Most importantly, they are all singular.

It seems as if the word *everyone* would be plural because it refers to a lot of people. But *everyone* refers to one group of people.

If you replace one of these words with another pronoun, you must use a singular pronoun such as *he* or *she*, not the plural pronouns *they* or *their*.

You will hear people replace a singular indefinite pronoun with the plural words *they* or *their* all the time:

Everyone sneezes when *they* have a cold.
Somebody left *their* lights on.
Did anybody lose *their* keys?

Even though these sentences sound fine, they are really not correct.

The following sentences are correct because the singular indefinite pronouns have been replaced by singular words:

Everyone sneezes when *he or she* has a cold.
Somebody left *his or her* lights on.
Did anybody lose *his or her* keys?

Perhaps the reason we have become so accustomed to using *they* and *their* is that *he or she* and *his or her* can sound awkward.

Here are three ways to write a smoother sentence and still use the correct pronouns:

First Method

If the indefinite pronoun is referring only to men or women, you can use just the masculine or feminine pronoun.

Coach speaking to NFL football players:
"Everybody should wear *his* red uniform."

Leader speaking to a Girl Scout troop:
"Anyone who wants to go should sign *her* name on the list."

Second Method

Keep the word *they* or *their* but replace the singular indefinite pronoun with a plural word, such as *people.*

Incorrect:	Everyone sneezes when they have a cold
Correct:	People sneeze when they have a cold.

Third Method

Revise the sentence to avoid the problem altogether.

Incorrect:	Somebody left their lights on.
Correct:	There is a red van in the parking lot with its lights on.

Incorrect:	Did anybody lose their keys?
Correct:	We found a set of keys in the break room.

Good news . . .

The rules about this are shifting. Some grammar books are starting to allow the use of **they** with singular indefinite pronouns. Until the time when everyone agrees to the new style, it's best to follow the traditional rule.

Pronouns with Compound Antecedents

Sometimes one pronoun can replace two names. When the two names are joined by *and*, the pronoun should be plural.

> Pam brushed *her* teeth.
> Pam and Sue brushed *their* teeth.
>
> Bill washed *his* car.
> Bill and Mike washed *their* cars.

When the two names are joined by *or* or *nor*, the pronoun should match the name closest to it in the sentence.

> Tom will bring *his* guitar.
> Either Tom or Tim will bring *his* guitar.
>
> The scouts couldn't find *their* way.
> The leader couldn't find *his* way.
> Neither the scouts nor the leader could find *his* way.
> Neither the leader nor the scouts could find *their* way.

As you can see, the last two sentences are essentially the same. The only difference is which antecedent is closest to the pronoun.

Try these and then check your answers below:

> Max and Sam rode (his – their) bikes to the store.
>
> Neither Max nor Sam brought (his – their) money.
>
> Either my boyfriend or his roommates will give up (his – their) Saturday to help me move.

Let's look at the first sentence:

> Max and Sam rode (his – their) bikes to the store.

What is the antecedent for this pronoun? *Max and Sam.*

Because we have the word *and* between the two names, we need to use the plural pronoun *their.*

> Max and Sam rode *their* bikes to the store.

Trick: If you know the antecedent is plural, but you're still not sure which pronoun to choose, try replacing the antecedent with the plural word *they.*

> *They* rode *their* bikes to the store.

Here's the second sentence:

> Neither Max nor Sam brought (his – their) money.

What is the antecedent? *Max nor Sam.*

Because the word *nor* comes between the names, match the pronoun to the name that is closest to the pronoun: *Sam.*

> Sam brought *his* money.
> Neither Max nor Sam brought *his* money.

Trick: If you know the antecedent is singular, but you're still not sure which pronoun to choose, try replacing the antecedent with the singular word *he.*

He brought *his* money.

Here's the third sentence:

> Either my boyfriend or his roommates will give up
> (his – their) Saturday to help me move.

What is the antecedent? *My boyfriend or his roommates.*

Because the word *or* comes between the names, match the pronoun to the name that is closest to the pronoun: *roommates.*

> His roommates will give up *their* Saturday.

> Either my boyfriend or his roommates will give up
> *their* Saturday to help me move.

Pronouns Separated from their Antecedents

Words that come in between the antecedent and the pronoun might cause you to choose the wrong pronoun.

> One of the tightrope walkers lost her balance.

Here the antecedent is *one.* One lost her balance. But the prepositional phrase *of the tightrope walkers* might throw you off. You might match the pronoun to *walkers:*

> One of the tightrope walkers lost their balance.

Putting parentheses around prepositional phrases can help you find the correct antecedent.

> One (of the tightrope walkers) lost *her* balance.
> Two (of the tightrope walkers) lost *their* balance.

Remember: A **preposition** is a word that tells what a cat can do with a chair: in, under, over, beside, etc.

A **prepositional phrase** is a group of words that starts with a preposition and then has a couple more words to complete the idea. For more details see page 25.

Exercise 6.2 Pronoun Agreement

Underline the antecedent and circle the correct pronoun. Check your answers on page 257.

1. Everybody should pack (his/her – their) suitcase before going to breakfast.

2. Sylvia and I got an early start on (her – our) holiday shopping.

3. Both Bill and Roger installed satellite dishes on (his – their) roofs.

4. Neither Bill nor Roger fell off (his – their) roof.

5. Two of the boys forgot (his – their) backpacks.

6. All employees must submit (his/her – their) expense reports by Friday.

7. Someone left (her – their) purse in the conference room.

8. Neither the professor nor the students could believe (his/her – their) eyes when the lab rat escaped.

9. Anyone who answers (his/her – their) cell phone during class will be counted absent.

10. One of the girls fell and skinned (her – their) knee.

Exercise 6.3 Pronoun Agreement

Underline the antecedent and circle the correct pronoun. Check your answers on page 258.

1. All students must pay (his/her – their) library fines by the end of the semester.

2. Both Sheila and Cindy got (her – their) hair done for graduation.

3. One of the students left (his/her – their) flash drive in the computer lab.

4. Everyone can pick up (his/her – their) paycheck on Friday.

5. Someone left (his – their) football helmet and pads in the locker room.

6. Three of the kids left (his/her – their) permission slips at home.

7. Both Cody and Dustin were late for (his – their) 8:00 classes.

8. Neither Cody nor Dustin heard (his – their) alarm clock.

9. Anyone who brings cookies to class will get extra credit on (his/her – their) quiz.

10. Either the coach or the players will tell the newscaster (his – their) thoughts about the game.

Subject–Verb Agreement

Just as a pronoun needs to agree with its antecedent, the subject and the verb of a sentence must agree with or match each other.

The rules for subject–verb agreement are identical to the rules for pronoun agreement.

Singular subjects take singular verbs:

Max eats candy.   Sue eats candy.

He eats candy.   She eats candy.

All these subjects are singular, just one person, and the verb *eats* sounds right.

Now let's look at some plural subjects that take plural verbs:

Max and Sue eat candy.   They eat candy.

With plural subjects, the verb *eat* sounds right.

Usually it is easy to choose the verb that will agree with its subject, but certain tricky situations can give writers trouble, and these are the same situations we learned about for pronoun agreement.

Hooray! One type of tricky situation that we WON'T have to deal with here is singular indefinite pronouns. Writers automatically use a singular verb with these subjects:

> Everyone **eats** candy.
> No one **eats** candy.

Subject–Verb Agreement with Compound Subjects

Sometimes two subjects share one verb. When the two subjects are joined by *and*, the subject is plural.

> <u>Bill</u> <u>washes</u> his car.
> <u>Tom</u> <u>washes</u> his car.
> <u>Bill</u> *and* <u>Tom</u> <u>wash</u> their cars.

When the two subjects are joined by *or* or *nor,* the verb should match the subject closest to it in the sentence:

> <u>Sam</u> <u>mows</u> my lawn every weekend.
> <u>Kevin</u> <u>mows</u> my lawn every weekend.
> Either <u>Sam</u> *or* <u>Kevin</u> <u>mows</u> my lawn every weekend.

> The <u>scouts</u> <u>were</u> not lost.
> The <u>leader</u> <u>was</u> not lost.
> Neither the <u>scouts</u> *nor* the <u>leader</u> <u>was</u> lost.
> Neither the <u>leader</u> *nor* the <u>scouts</u> <u>were</u> lost.

As you can see, the last two sentences are essentially the same. The only difference is which subject is closest to the verb.

Try these and then check your answers below:

> Justin and Patrick (go – goes) to every home game.
>
> Neither Joan nor Deirdre (drinks – drink) coffee.
>
> Either Jasmine or her sisters (visits – visit) Grandma once a week.

Let's look at the first sentence:

> Justin and Patrick (go – goes) to every home game.

What is the subject for this verb? *Justin and Patrick.*

Because we have the word *and* between the two names, the subject is plural:

> <u>Justin</u> and <u>Patrick</u> <u>go</u> to every home game.

Trick: If you know the subject is plural, replace the names with the plural word *they*. Then you can hear which verb sounds right:

> <u>They</u> <u>go</u> to every home game.

Here's the second sentence:

> Neither Joan nor Deirdre (drinks – drink) coffee.

What is the subject? *Joan nor Deirdre.* Because the word *nor* comes between the two names, match the verb to the subject that is closest to it: *Deirdre.*

Deirdre <u>drinks</u> coffee.
Neither Joan nor <u>Deirdre</u> <u>drinks</u> coffee.

Trick: If you know the subject is singular, replace the name with the singular word *he* or *she*. Then you can hear which verb sounds right:

<u>She</u> <u>drinks</u> coffee.

Here's the third sentence:

Either Jasmine or her sisters (visits – visit) Grandma once a week.

What is the subject? *Jasmine or her sisters.*

Because the word *or* comes between the subjects, match the verb with the subject that is closest to it: *sisters.*

<u>Sisters</u> <u>visit</u> Grandma once a week.

Either Jasmine or her <u>sisters</u> <u>visit</u> Grandma once a week.

Subjects Separated from the Verbs

Words that come in between the subject and the verb might cause you to choose the wrong verb.

Every day <u>one</u> of the football players <u>falls</u> down.

Here the subject is one—one falls down. But the prepositional phrase *of the football players* might cause you to match the verb to *players:*

Every day <u>one</u> of the football players <u>fall</u> down.

A word in a prepositional phrase will not be the subject. Putting parentheses around the prepositional phrase can help you find the correct subject.

<u>One</u> (of the football players) <u>falls</u> down.
<u>Three</u> (of the football players) <u>fall</u> down.

Remember: A **preposition** is a word that tells what a cat can do with a chair: in, under, over, beside, etc.

A **prepositional phrase** is a group of words that starts with a preposition and then has a couple more words to complete the idea. For more details see page 25.

Exercise 6.4 Subject–Verb Agreement

Underline the subject; then circle the correct verb. Check your answers on page 258.

1. Jennifer and Nicole (meets – <u>meet</u>) at the Suds-n-Bubbles Laundromat every Monday to wash their clothes.

2. Either Jennifer or Nicole (<u>brings</u> – bring) magazines to read while doing the laundry.

3. All of Aunt Sadie's prize rose bushes (was – were) completely covered with aphids.

4. One of the rose bushes (was – were) still blooming, however.

5. Neither the employees nor the manager (knows – know) how to install a new roll of paper into the cash register.

6. Red Lobster and Olive Garden (is – are) my favorite restaurants.

7. Neither Red Lobster nor Olive Garden (takes – take) reservations.

8. Olive Garden, one of the best Italian restaurants, (serves – serve) great spaghetti.

9. Red Lobster, which has a huge tank full of lobsters, (offers – offer) fresh seafood.

10. Both Red Lobster and Olive Garden (has – have) wonderful desserts.

Exercise 6.5 Subject—Verb Agreement

Underline the subject; then circle the correct verb. Check your answers on page 259.

1. Megan and her friends (works – work) at Starbucks.

2. Either Megan or her friends (takes – take) orders from the customers.

3. Neither Megan nor the other employees (wants – want) to take out the trash.

4. Megan, the newest of the employees, (has – have) to do this nasty job.

5. The dumpster, which is in an alley full of trash cans, (smells – smell) terrible.

6. Jasmine, one of Megan's co-workers, (gives – give) Megan a sympathetic smile.

7. Before Megan got hired, Jasmine (was – were) the one taking out the trash.

8. Megan and her friends (enjoys – enjoy) preparing the drinks.

9. The coffee and tea (smells – smell) wonderful.

10. One of Megan's favorite drinks (is – are) a skinny mocha.

Chapter Seven

Powerful Writing

This chapter gets into smaller details for making your writing more powerful. If your papers have problems with misplaced or dangling modifiers, you could be writing something funny that you didn't intend to say. We will also cover passive voice, wordiness, and parallel structure. These problems are easy to fix once you become aware of them.

Modifiers

A **modifier** is a word or group of words that describes or gives details.

> I have a red car.

Here the modifier is the word *red* which is describing the car. Different languages have different rules about where the modifier needs to go. The French version looks like this:

J'ai une voiture rouge.
I have a car red.

This sounds funny because the modifier is not in the usual place for English. Most of the time we automatically put the modifier in the correct place. Two kinds of mistakes that writers may make are **misplaced modifiers** and **dangling modifiers**.

> ### Getting tricky . . .
>
> An **adjective** is a word that modifies (describes) a noun or pronoun. An **adverb** is a word that modifies (describes) a verb, an adjective, or another adverb.
>
> For more information on adjectives and adverbs, see pages 233 and 234.

Misplaced Modifiers

A modifier placed too far away from the word it is trying to modify is called a **misplaced modifier**. You may have heard this joke from the movie *Mary Poppins*:

> I know a man with a wooden leg named Smith.
> Really? And what is the name of his other leg?

If the modifier *named Smith* is too far away from the word it is trying to modify—*man*—the sentence sounds as if his leg was named Smith.

Rearrange the words so that the modifier is closer to the word it is really modifying:

I know a man named Smith with a wooden leg.

A **split infinitive** is a particular kind of misplaced modifier. An infinitive is the word *to* followed by a verb. Don't put any words in between the *to* and the verb.

I try *to* always *tell* the truth.	split infinitive
I always try *to tell* the truth.	correct
Be sure *to* never *break* a promise.	split infinitive
Be sure never *to break* a promise.	correct
Never break a promise.	correct

The times they are a-changin'...

The rule about split infinitives is fading away. Most grammar books don't even mention it anymore.

For more on infinitives, see page 215.

Dangling Modifiers

A **dangling modifier** occurs when the word that the modifier is trying to modify does not even appear in the sentence.

As a young girl, her father taught her to climb trees.

The modifier is *as a young girl*, but who was a young girl? We don't have a girl's name in this sentence. It almost sounds as if her father used to be a young girl!

Revise this sentence carefully. It is not enough to say

> As a young girl, Sally's father taught her to climb trees.

This still sounds as if *as a young girl* is modifying *father*. Here are two correct versions:

> As a young girl, Sally climbed trees with her father.
> When Sally was a young girl, her father taught her to climb trees.

Exercise 7.1 Misplaced and Dangling Modifiers

Rewrite these sentences to solve the modifier problems.

Check your answers on page 260.

1. I loaned my wool sweater to Jackie with the red stripes.

2. To save electricity, remember to always turn down the thermostat when you leave the house.

3. The museum curator showed the new painting to the guests hanging on the wall.

4. Walking quickly, the convenience store is about ten minutes away.

5.   The doctor suggested a new treatment for my in-grown toenail that is painless.

6.   Patrick promised to never leave the milk out overnight again.

7.   Sara ordered a bagel from the waitress with cream cheese.

8.   Eating tacos, the salsa dripped all over my hands.

9.   While studying for my history exam, my roommate turned on the tv.

10.   The dentist told Kevin to always floss his teeth.

Passive vs. Active Voice

Remember—To find the verb in a sentence, say *yesterday, every day,* and *tomorrow* at the beginning of the sentence and then listen for the word that changes.

> *Yesterday* the bank **was robbed** by Felix.
> *Every day* the bank **is robbed** by Felix.
> *Tomorrow* the bank **will be robbed** by Felix.

To find the subject, ask "Who or what performed the verb?"

> Who or what was robbed by Felix? *bank*
> The <u>bank</u> <u>was robbed</u> by Felix.

See Chapter 1 for more details on finding verbs and subjects.

> ## Getting tricky . . .
>
> In the sentence about Felix, **was robbed** is the verb even though the word **robbed** didn't change when we changed the time. For practical purposes it works just fine to mark only the word that actually changes: **was.**
>
> If you want to delve in and learn about helping verbs and verb phrases, see page 212.

Passive voice is when the subject of the sentence is not the person who actually did the verb.

> The bank was robbed by Felix.

The verb is *was robbed.* To find the subject, we ask, "Who or what was robbed?" The answer, *bank,* is the subject.

Now ask yourself, "Did the subject actually do the verb? Did the bank do the robbing?" No. Who actually did the robbing? *Felix.*

But *Felix* is not the subject of the sentence. That's why this sentence is in **passive voice.**

Passive voice is not grammatically incorrect, but it sounds weak. It's usually best to use active voice when possible.

Turning a passive sentence into **active voice** is easy: just move the words around so that the person who actually did the verb is the subject:

Felix <u>robbed</u> the bank.

Let's try another sentence.

The <u>juice was spilled</u> by Susan.

The verb is *was spilled*. "Who or what was spilled by Susan?"

The answer, *juice*, is the subject.

"Did the subject actually do the verb? Did the juice spill anything?" No. "Who spilled it?" *Susan*

The active voice version of this sentence looks like this:

<u>Susan spilled</u> the juice.

Here's one more example:

The <u>award was won</u> by Serena.

The verb is *was won*. "Who or what was won by Serena?"

The answer, *award*, is the subject.

"Did the award win anything?" No. "Who actually won it?" *Serena.*

The active voice version of this sentence looks like this:

<u>Serena won</u> the award.

Sometimes passive voice is the best choice. What if you don't know who robbed the bank?

The <u>bank</u> <u>was robbed</u>!!

This is passive voice because the subject *bank* did not actually do the robbing. You could still write this sentence as active voice by saying

<u>Somebody</u> <u>robbed</u> the bank!!

Exercise 7.2 Passive Voice

Rewrite each sentence in active voice. If the passive sentence does not say who performed the verb, use *someone* as the subject in your active voice sentence. Check your answers on page 261.

EXAMPLE: The pool was cleaned last week.

Someone cleaned the pool last week.

1. The brownies were eaten by Sandy.

2. King Louis XVI was beheaded in Paris in 1793.

3. The dishes were washed by George.

4. A buried treasure chest was dug up by the pirate.

5. The incorrect statistics were released by a member of the committee.

6. Three priceless paintings were found in a storage unit.

7. The new construction project was approved by the board.

8. The faulty valve had been inspected two months earlier.

9. Tickets will be taken by the ushers.

10. The new movie will be released on October 1.

Avoiding Wordiness

Writing that uses many more words than really needed is called **wordy**:

> After the end of the final curtain call, we exited the theater, went outside, and walked down the sidewalk to a little, small, cozy restaurant café.

Some of the words in this sentence repeat what has already been said: *little, small, cozy*. Other words aren't needed. A shorter version is easier to read and more powerful because it expresses the same idea with fewer words:

> When the play ended, we walked to a cozy restaurant.

Many writers will use unnecessary words when they write a rough draft because they are trying to figure out what they want to say. When you revise your rough draft, be sure to eliminate those unnecessary words.

Also, writers may use extra words in an attempt to sound formal and sophisticated. Usually it's better to say what you mean succinctly and clearly while still maintaining an appropriate level of formality.

> Due to the fact that my purse is empty and devoid of any money, either paper or coin, I must decline your invitation to the cinema movie theater and satisfy myself with watching video entertainment on my television for the present time until the occasion arises that I once again enjoy the abundance of funds for discretionary usage.

The shorter version is still formal, but it is much easier for the reader to understand:

> Unfortunately, I must decline your invitation because I do not have sufficient funds in my entertainment budget at this time.

Exercise 7.3 Revising Wordiness

Rewrite the following passage to eliminate unnecessary words and make the instructions easier to understand. One possible answer is given on page 262.

In the event that the engine of the lawn and yard mower fails to start or begin running following a quick, swift, and rapid pulling action upon the mower's starting cord, the owner of the mower who is making an attempt to bring the mower's engine into a running condition would be advised to use any of his or her fingers or thumbs to push down upon and press the mower's primer button several times in rapid succession so that upon a second attempt at pulling the cord the owner and user of the lawn and yard mower might experience increased probability of a successful outcome to a subsequent quick, swift, and rapid pull upon the mower's starting cord.

Parallel Structure

Why does the following sentence sound awkward?

Sam mowed the grass and trimming the shrubs.

This sentence tells two things that Sam did, but the two things are not presented in a parallel way: **mowed** doesn't match with **trimming.** This type of mistake is called faulty parallelism. Correct faulty parallelism by choosing words that match:

Sam mowed the grass and trimmed the shrubs.

Not Parallel
Sam wants to   mow the grass,
trim the shrubs, and
raking the leaves.

Parallel
Sam wants to   mow the grass,
trim the shrubs, and
rake the leaves.

Not Parallel

Sam wants

to mow the grass,
to trim the shrubs, and
raking the leaves.

Parallel

Sam wants

to mow the grass,
to trim the shrubs, and
to rake the leaves.

Not Parallel

Sam was

mowing the grass,
trimming the shrubs, and
to rake the leaves.

Parallel

Sam was

mowing the grass,
trimming the shrubs, and
raking the leaves.

Not Parallel

Sam trimmed

the rose bushes,
the holly bushes, and
hydrangeas

Parallel

Sam trimmed

the rose bushes,
the holly bushes, and
the hydrangea bushes.

Not Parallel

Sam trimmed

the roses,
the hollies, and
the hydrangea bushes.

Parallel

Sam trimmed
the roses,
the hollies, and
the hydrangeas.

Not Parallel

Sam raked
under the trees,
around the swingset, and
the house.

Parallel

Sam raked
under the trees,
around the swingset, and
beside the house.

Not Parallel

Sam got
hot,
sweaty, and
he was thirsty.

Parallel

Sam got
hot,
sweaty, and
thirsty.

Exercise 7.4 Practice with Parallel Structure

Rewrite each sentence to fix any problems with parallelism. Check your answers on page 262.

EXAMPLE:

Sally enjoys watching movies, reading books, and to go to the mall.

Sally enjoys watching movies, reading books, and ***going*** to the mall.

1. In the attic, I found a broken typewriter, an old suit-case, and a doll house that was dusty.

2. Scott was voted player of the year for his speed, con-centration, and his ability to lead.

3. Florida is a popular vacation spot because it has theme parks, beaches, and the weather is great.

4. Jan's new job pays well, has great benefits, and she gets two weeks of vacation.

5. The mouse ran across the kitchen floor, behind the re-frigerator, and there was a hole that he went into.

6. The movie was dramatic and with lots of excitement.

7. Patricia went to the grocery store, the dry cleaners, and stopped at the bank.

8. The library smelled like mildew, dust, and like old books.

9. During spring break, Jake wants to go to the beach, eat lots of seafood, and getting a tan.

10. The flight attendants were cheerful, friendly, and with smiles.

Chapter Eight

Homophones

Homophone means "same sound." Homophones (also called homonyms) are words that sound the same but are spelled differently and have different meanings.

Teachers will often mark a homophone error as **wrong word** because you didn't really make a spelling mistake; you just wrote a word that was different from the word you meant.

General Homophones

accept	I accept your apology.
except	Joan remembered everything except her camera.
advice	My uncle gives me good advice.
advise	I would advise you not to eat that moldy cheese.
	*In **advise**, the S sounds like a Z.*

affect	The soggy field might affect the team's performance.
	Affect is a verb.
effect	Jason said his daily run was having a good effect on his health.
	Effect is a noun.

For more on nouns and verbs, see pages 228 and 229.

a lot	Movie stars receive a lot of fan mail.
	A lot is two separate words.
allot	Dad will allot me $20 per week.
	Allot means give.
already	That test was easy. I am already finished.
all ready	We were all ready to go by six o'clock.
are	We are going to the zoo.
our	This is our house.
bare	I like to feel the grass under my bare feet.
bear	Lucy has a stuffed teddy bear.
	I can't bear to see you cry.

bored	On rainy days, little children get bored.
board	We were the last ones to board the plane.
	Steve cut the board in half with his saw.
break	Be careful not to break anything.
	Every two hours, you get a ten-minute break.
brake	Hit the brake! There's a stop sign!
buy	I'm saving my money to buy a car.
by	I have a night light by my bed.
capitol	Her office is in the state capitol building.
capital	Raleigh is the capital city of North Carolina.
coarse	Coarse sandpaper is very rough.
course	Gerry teaches the piano course.
	On Saturdays, the golf course is crowded.
compliment	Mary's date gave her a compliment.
complement	David chose a tie to complement his suit.

conscience	Do you have a guilty conscience?
conscious	Jim was unconscious after the accident.
dairy	Milk is in the dairy section.
diary	Becky writes in her diary every day.
every day	Debbie makes her bed every day.
everyday	These are my everyday shoes. *Everyday means ordinary or common.*
forth	The explorers went forth into the wilderness.
fourth	Elizabeth is in fourth grade.
fare	To ride the bus, you must pay a dollar fare.
fair	Divide the work equally so that it will be fair. Every fall, Scott goes to the county fair. Jill gets sunburned easily because she is fair.
herd	A group of cattle is called a herd.
heard	I just heard the good news!

here	When will Marcus be here?
	Here is that CD I borrowed.
hear	Please talk louder. I can't hear you.
horse	A cowboy rides a horse.
hoarse	Jamie yelled until her voice was hoarse.
its	The cat chased its ball.
it's	It's a hot day today.
	It's** is a contraction of **it is.

For a review of contractions, turn to page 79.

lay and lie	turn to page 146.
led	Sue led me to the surprise party.
lead	Lead is a kind of metal.
	In ballroom dancing, the man will lead.

For this meaning, lead is pronounced LEED.

loose	These pants are too loose and baggy.
lose	Don't lose your gloves.
meat	Mary doesn't eat meat; she's a vegetarian
meet	Would you like to meet my roommate?

no	No, I don't like tomatoes.
know	Do you know how to change a flat tire?
past	History teaches stories from the past.
passed	Oh no! We just passed the house! Sally passed the class with a B.
patience	Teaching preschool requires a lot of patience.
patients	The nurse cared for five patients.
piece	May I have another piece of cake please?
peace	Sue enjoyed an hour of peace and quiet.
plane	Have you ever ridden on an airplane? Carpenters use a plane to shave wood.
plain	I'll have my cake plain, no ice cream. A big, grassy area is called a plain.
presents	Vanessa received five presents for Christmas.
presence	Shawn appreciated his mother's presence while he was in the hospital.

principal	Mr. Shawnessy is the principal of the school.
principle	A minister should have good principles.
rain	There is a ten percent chance of rain today.
rein	When you ride a horse, hold the reins firmly.
reign	The reign of Elizabeth I was the Golden Age.
right	At the next intersection, turn right. I believe I got all the answers right.
write	Denise likes to write poetry.
rode	I rode a horse around the corral.
road	Look both ways before you cross the road.
scene	I enjoyed a beautiful scene of the ocean. A play is divided into acts and scenes.
seen	Have you seen my jacket?
sense	That theory just doesn't make any sense. I have an excellent sense of smell.
since	Since I mowed the lawn, I have been resting.

than	Zack is taller than Zoe.
then	Let's wash the dishes; then we can watch tv.
their	My neighbors love their new dog.
there	There are three frogs in the pond.
	The bathrooms are over there.
they're	They're driving to Florida this summer. ***They're** is a contraction of **they are**.*

For a review of contractions, turn to page 79.

through	Let's drive through the park.
threw	The pitcher threw a curve ball.
to	I'm going to the store to buy some shoes.
two	I will also buy two new dresses.
too	Is that too much to spend in one day?
	Would you like to come too?
	***Too** means also or an excessive amount.*
waste	Don't waste electricity.
waist	The pirate wore a red sash around his waist.

wear	What should I wear today?
where	Where is my hair brush?
week	My birthday is one week from today.
weak	I do push-ups so I'll be strong, not weak.
were	We were stuck in traffic for two hours!
we're	We're going to the movies.

We're *is a contraction of* **we are.**

whether	I wonder whether it will rain.
weather	The weather is perfect for a picnic.

who and whom turn to page 147.

whose	Whose turn is it to clean the bathroom?
who's	Do you know who's going to be at the party?

Who's *is a contraction of* **who is.**

your	This is your glass of lemonade.
you're	You're supposed to call after 2 p.m.

You're *is a contraction of* **you are.**

For a review of contractions, turn to page 79.

Lay and Lie

These words are tricky because their meanings are quite similar and the tenses overlap. The past tense of the verb *lie* is the same word as the present tense of the verb *lay*.

The verb *lie* means to recline your body:

> *Every day* I **lie** down and take a nap.
> *Tomorrow* I **will lie** down and take a nap.
> *Yesterday* I **lay** down and took a nap.

> *Every day* he **lies** down and takes a nap.
> *Tomorrow* he **will lie** down and take a nap.
> *Yesterday* he **lay** down and took a nap.

The verb *lay* means to place an object:

> *Every day* I **lay** my keys on the kitchen table.
> *Tomorrow* I **will lay** my keys on the kitchen table.
> *Yesterday* I **laid** my keys on the kitchen table.

> *Every day* she **lays** her keys on the kitchen table.
> *Tomorrow* she **will lay** her keys on the kitchen table.
> *Yesterday* she **laid** her keys on the kitchen table.

> **Of course . . .**
>
> Lay and lie have other meanings too:
>
> Tell the truth; don't lie.
>
> Chickens lay eggs.

Who and Whom

This one is really difficult. To understand the intricacies of *who* and *whom,* you would need to do an extensive study of traditional grammar which is beyond the scope of what most people need to know in order to write correctly. In fact, *whom* is disappearing from the language and is rarely used except in very formal writing.

The following method for *who* and *whom* works well in most cases.

Use *who* when you could answer the question with *she, he* or *they*:

> Who won the race?
> She won the race.
>
> The prize went to the person who finished first.
> Who finished first?
> He finished first.

Who can be calling so late at night?
They can be calling so late at night.

I forgot who is supposed to do the dishes tonight.
Who is supposed to do the dishes tonight?
She is supposed to do the dishes tonight.

Use *whom* when you could answer the question with *her, him,* or *them:*

The partner whom I was assigned to was terrible.
Whom was I assigned to?
I was assigned to him.

The producer is Ms. Spencer whom you will be
working with closely.
Whom will you be working with closely?
You will be working with her.

Whom did the victim identify as the robber?
The victim identified him as the robber.

With whom did you hike last summer?
You hiked with them last summer.

Chapter Nine

Sentence Types

This chapter teaches the steps for identifying the four different types of sentences: simple, compound, complex, and compound-complex.

People write all four types of sentences even though they may not know what the sentences are called. Because the smoothest, most interesting writing uses a mixture of sentences, a conscious awareness of the four types can help you improve your writing style as well as your punctuation.

Remember—An **independent clause** has a subject and a verb, and it expresses a complete idea.

> <u>Mario</u> <u>hit</u> the winning run   IC
> the <u>weather</u> <u>was</u> cold   IC

A **dependent clause** also has a subject and a verb, but it leaves the reader hanging. A dependent clause begins with a **subordinating conjunction** that changes the sound of the clause.

<u>after</u> <u>Mario</u> <u>hit</u> the winning run . . . what?   DC
<u>although</u> <u>the</u> <u>weather</u> <u>was</u> cold . . . what?   DC

A **phrase** is any group of words that does not have a subject and a verb.

in the morning   Ph
<u>wore</u> a blue suit   Ph

For more information on clauses, phrases, and subordinating conjunctions, see pages 21–29.

Common Subordinating Conjunctions

after	although	as	because
before	if	since	so that
that	though	till	until
unless	when	where	while

The Four Sentence Types

Phrases, dependent clauses, and independent clauses are the building blocks that we use to make the four different types of sentences.

We analyze sentence type by counting how many independent clauses and how many dependent clauses a sentence has. Phrases don't matter.

A **simple sentence** has only one clause—an independent clause. Mark simple sentences **S.**

Josephine <u>wore</u> a purple velvet gown.
　　　IC

(At the New Year's Eve Ball), Josephine <u>wore</u> a
　　　　　　　Ph　　　　　　　　　　　　　IC

purple velvet gown (with a satin cape).
　　　　　　　　　　　　Ph

The second sentence is much longer because it has two phrases. But it is still a simple sentence because it has only one clause.

A **compound sentence** has two (or more) independent clauses. Mark compound sentences **CP.**

Philip <u>saw</u> Josephine; <u>he</u> <u>asked</u> her to dance.
　IC　　　　　　　　　　　IC

Philip <u>saw</u> Josephine (in her purple gown); (with a
　IC　　　　　　　　　　　　Ph　　　　　　　　　Ph

nervous voice) <u>he</u> <u>asked</u> her to dance.
　　　　　　　　　IC

The second sentence is much longer because it has two phrases. But it is still a compound sentence because it has two independent clauses.

A **complex sentence** has one independent clause and one (or more) dependent clauses. It doesn't matter whether the dependent clause comes first or last. Mark complex sentences **CX.**

After <u>they</u> <u>danced</u>, <u>they</u> <u>drank</u> champagne.
　DC　　　　　　　IC

<u>They</u> <u>drank</u> champagne after <u>they</u> <u>danced</u>.
　IC　　　　　　　　　　　DC

If the dependent clause comes first, put a comma after it. If the independent clause comes first, don't put a comma. See page 51 for more information.

A **compound-complex sentence** has at least three clauses. Like a complex sentence, it has at least one dependent clause. Like a compound sentence, it has two (or more) independent clauses. It doesn't matter what order the clauses are in. Mark compound-complex sentences **CPX**.

> When the ball ended, Philip took Josephine (to a
>   DC   IC
> restaurant), and they dined (on truffles and caviar).
>   Ph   IC   Ph

Steps for Analyzing Sentence Types

1. Double Underline the Verbs

2. Underline the Subjects

3. Count the Clauses One clause—mark it **S for simple** More than one clause—go on to the next step

4. Are there any subordinating conjunctions? No—mark it **CP for compound** Yes—draw a wavy line under them—go on to the next step

5. How many independent clauses are there? One— mark it **CX for complex** Two or more—**CPX for compound-complex**

> ### Getting tricky . . .
>
> See page 224 to learn about relative clauses that count as dependent clauses in analyzing sentence type.

Exercise 9.1 Analyzing Sentence Types

Follow the steps and identify the type for each sentence. Check your answers on page 262.

EXAMPLE:

Following her junior year in college, <u>Chelsea</u> <u>traveled</u> to Europe for the summer; <u>Jordan</u> <u>remained</u> on campus.   **CP**

1. After Chelsea left, Jordan found himself bored and restless.

2. He spent several days watching TV and playing video games.

3. Chelsea sent him pictures of the Globe Theatre and Big Ben, and he sent her pictures of his cactus and the empty basketball court.

4. One day Jordan walked the entire campus, discovering numerous new buildings.

5. The next day he returned to the Career Center where he found job postings and internship opportunities.

6. Chelsea, meanwhile, sent pictures of the Eiffel Tower.

7. When Jordan found a local company looking for an intern in their accounting department, he e-mailed to ask about the position; they immediately replied that they had a sudden opening.   C P X

8. The previous intern left in disgrace after he spilled coffee on the computer.

9. Jordan spent the next six weeks as an intern. S

10. At the end of the summer, Chelsea had numerous adventures in Europe to share, and Jordan had an internship experience for his résumé.

Exercise 9.2 Analyzing Sentence Types

Follow the steps and identify the type for each sentence. Check your answers on page 263.

EXAMPLE: Elephants are called pachyderms; this means "thick skinned."

1. Because they eat a lot of vegetation, elephants travel long distances. C X

2. In just one day, an average elephant will eat over three hundred pounds of vegetation. S

3. Elephants grow up to twelve feet tall, and they weigh up to fourteen hundred pounds. C P

4. Elephants have the largest brain of any animal; a typical elephant brain is four times as large as a human brain.

5. An elephant's trunk is very sensitive because it contains forty thousand muscles; an elephant can pick up a small coin with its trunk.

6. Although predators will kill baby elephants, adult elephants are typically safe from all predators except humans.

7. Despite their reputation for never forgetting anything, elephants remember things only as well as other animals like cats and dogs.

8. The white elephant gift originated in ancient Asia where ordinary elephants were common, but white elephants were rare.

9. Since white elephants were sacred, the unlucky owner of a white elephant had to feed it special food and welcome the elephant's many visitors.

10. No one wanted to receive a white elephant as a gift.

Tricky Details in Analyzing Sentence Types

Compound Verbs and Subjects—Counting the clauses can be tricky if a clause has a compound verb or a compound subject or both. Consider the difference between these two sentences:

Sue and Joe cooked dinner and washed the dishes.
Sue cooked dinner, and Joe washed the dishes.

The first sentences has a compound subject (Sue and Joe) and a compound verb (cooked and washed). Both people did both things. The structure is subject – subject – verb – verb. This is just one clause!

In the second sentence the structure is different: subject – verb – subject – verb. Sue didn't wash the dishes, and Joe didn't cook. This sentence has two clauses!

Here's how you should mark these two sentences:

Sue and Joe cooked dinner and washed the dishes.   **S**

Sue cooked dinner, and Joe washed the dishes.   **CP**

False Subordinating Conjunctions

Usually it is easy to find subordinating conjunctions. You can simply look at the first word of a clause, and if that word is on the list of subordinating conjunctions, you draw a wavy line under it.

After Jamie rode the Zipper, her stomach was upset.
       DC   IC

In this sentence, the word *after* makes the first clause dependent:

After Jamie rode the Zipper . . . what happened?

The first clause depends on the second (independent) clause to finish the idea.

But the word *after* is not always a subordinating conjunction.

> After riding the Zipper, <u>Jamie</u> <u>had</u> an upset stomach.
> IC

This sentence has only one clause. Is the word *after* making the clause dependent? When you say the sentence out loud, does it sound as if you need to keep talking to finish the idea? No. This sentence sounds finished. The word *after* is not making the clause dependent, so *after* is not working as a subordinating conjunction in this sentence.

So don't rely only on your eyes to identify subordinating conjunctions. Use your ears too. If you see a word that is on the list of subordinating conjunctions, read that clause out loud to hear if it sounds unfinished. If the clause sounds unfinished, you know that it is a dependent clause and the first word of the clause is functioning as a subordinating conjunction.

Getting tricky . . .

If **after** isn't a subordinating conjunction in this sentence, what is it?

After is part of a phrase that functions as an adverb. For an explanation of adverbs, see page 234.

Exercise 9.3 Tricky Sentence Types

Follow the steps to analyze these sentences. Look out for compound subjects and verbs. Before you draw any wavy lines, make sure that word is really doing the job of a subordinating conjunction. Write **S, CP, CX,** or **CPX.** Check your answers on page 264.

1. Zork and Zink were aliens from the planet Zigland.

2. Because they were scientists, they wanted to visit Earth, so they traveled nearly a billion miles.

3. When they landed on Earth, they were astonished by the colors.

4. On Zigland the grass is purple, and the sky looks yellow.

5. After climbing down from their space ship, Zork and Zink went exploring.

6. They gathered plant specimens and took water samples.

7. Although they wanted to interview some animals, they failed to make sense of the animals' noises.

8. Since Zork and Zink were the size of mice, a stray cat chased and cornered them; she hoped for a new lunch meat.

9. The tiny scientists immediately beamed themselves back to their ship and took off for Zigland.

10. After returning to Zigland with their samples, they received a hero's welcome.

Common Subordinating Conjunctions

after	although	as	because
before	if	since	so that
that	though	till	until
unless	when	where	while

Chapter Ten

Research Skills

Most students will need to write many different types of research papers during college. An art history professor, a chemistry professor, and a psychology professor will assign very different research assignments; however, every research assignment will require you to use the research skills covered in this chapter.

The following example is a short research paper for a literature class, but the skills needed for writing this paper are the same research skills a student would need for writing a ten page paper on World War I or a twenty page paper on photosynthesis.

As you read this paper, consider how it is more complicated than other types of essays, and think about what additional tasks the student had to perform to complete it.

Jane Doe

Professor Jones

English 111

20 April 2013

Charles Dickens

Poverty, Success, and Social Justice

When Charles Dickens was born to a struggling, working-class family in 1812, no one dreamed that he would become a wealthy British novelist and author of classic books including *Oliver Twist*, *Great Expectations*, *A Christmas Carol*, and *David Copperfield* (Cody). Since many of the events and characters in his books were taken from his own life experiences, his poor background shaped his writing as well as his personality.

Dickens' father was a clerk; his mother was of "slightly higher social class" ("Dickens"). His poor but stable family life changed suddenly when he was twelve years old. Dickens' father was sent to London's Marshalsea Prison for Debtors, and Dickens had to quit school and get a job working in a factory (Haines 6–8). His miserable experience at the factory "haunted him all of his life" and left him "scarred psychologically" (Cody).

Then, miraculously, his father received a large inheritance, left prison, and sent Dickens back to school. After finishing school at age fifteen, Dickens held various jobs including clerk for a solicitor (lawyer) and newspaper typist. He began selling stories to magazines and newspapers in 1833. In 1836 a collection of his stories was published as his first book ("Dickens"). He began writing his first novel, *Oliver Twist,* in 1837 (Cody).

In the following years, Dickens wrote many novels and became famous. He used his fame to try to change society by writing about the lives of the poor. Most of his middle and upper class readers had no idea that people were treated so unfairly. In time, Dickens became wealthy, and his used his money to help others:

> He was a major philanthropist who expertly used his name and his time to draw attention to the scandalous condition of the poor. He took pity on children whose education he paid for and anonymously sent money to desperate men and women, including prisoners . . . .
> (Smith)

At the same time, Dickens' hard childhood made him "insecure emotionally" (Cody). He showed off by wearing expensive, flashy clothes such as "gold chains and rings, and flamboyantly colored waistcoats [vests]" ("Dickens"). He treated his wife, Catherine, terribly. After she gave birth to their third son, Dickens refused to see the baby, and he criticized Catherine for getting fat. Since divorce was not allowed at that time, they separated, and Dickens said, "That figure is out of my life for evermore . . ." (qtd. in Smith).

Dickens' health suffered from his busy schedule of writing and promoting his books. After a trip to America, he returned home exhausted, his health "permanently broken" ("Dickens"). He continued writing until he was fifty-eight when he died of a stroke (Haines 165–67).

Dickens' childhood of poverty and humiliation had good and bad effects. While it led him to be insecure and sometimes cruel, it also made him compassionate, "a champion of the oppressed" ("Dickens"). His descriptions of suffering and injustice raised the consciousness of his readers which helped improve life for working people of England.

Works Cited

Cody, David. "Dickens: A Brief Biography." *The Victorian Web: Literature, History, and Culture in the Age of Victoria.* N.p. Mar. 2004. Web. 27 Dec. 2011.

"Dickens, Charles." *British Authors of the Nineteenth Century.* Ed. Stanley J. Kunitz. New York: Wilson, 1936. Print.

Haines, Charles. *Charles Dickens.* New York: Franklin Watts, 1969. Print.

Smith, Kyle. "Humbug!" *New York Post.* Review of *Charles Dickens: A Life* by Claire Tomalin. *NYPost.com.* 24 Dec. 2011. Web. 25 Dec. 2011.

Besides the usual steps involved in writing an essay, when you write a research paper, you must perform three additional tasks:

1. **Do research** to find the information that you will need.

    The section on research begins on page 168.

2. **Take notes** by reading your sources and then rewriting the information in your own words (paraphrasing) and copying some exact words (quoting).

    Notetaking begins on page 171.

    Paraphrasing begins on page 175.

    Quoting begins on page 182.

3. **Document** your information in two ways:

    Use **parenthetical notes** (also called in-text citations) throughout the essay.

    Include a **list of works cited** on a separate page at the end of your paper.

    Parenthetical notes begin on page 189.

    The list of works cited begins on page 201.

Different Styles for Documenting Research

There are several different formats a writer can use to document the sources in a research paper. This book shows the MLA (Modern Language Association) style which is used in English and most humanities classes. APA (American Psychological Association) is another popular style which is often used for science and social science classes. Many history professors prefer Chicago or Turabian style. Each of these styles is different in small ways, but they all have the same purpose: to show the reader where the information came from. Once you understand MLA documentation, it is not too difficult to switch to a different format. You can look in a reference book or online source and follow the examples given for that style.

Plagiarism

Plagiarism means pretending that you wrote something that you didn't really write. Extreme plagiarism would be taking an entire essay off the internet and putting your name on it. A more common type of plagiarism happens when students aren't careful with their paraphrasing, quoting, and documentation. The consequences for all types of plagiarism are often severe. Follow the guidelines in this chapter for paraphrasing, quoting, and documenting, and you can write a strong paper without plagiarism.

Doing Research

Doing research can seem like an overwhelming task. Where do you begin? If you type "Charles Dickens" into a search engine, you will have thirty-one million hits to sort through. By typing "Charles Dickens' Life" you will reduce the results to twenty-three million hits. Then there are the many books and articles about Charles Dickens that can be found in public and college libraries. Obviously, sifting through all that information will take too long. You will need to narrow your topic.

To narrow your topic, start by doing *preliminary research*: look through encyclopedias and other reference sources to get a general overview of your topic. Which aspects of the topic are most interesting to you? As Jane did her preliminary research, she noticed that many of the sources mentioned that Dickens' father was sent to a debtors' prison and Dickens had to leave school and work in a factory. Jane was interested in how this experience affected Dickens' life and his writing. She decided to focus on this aspect of Dickens' life for her paper.

After you have narrowed your topic, the next step is to develop a *research question*. What question do you want to answer in your paper? Jane's research question was, "How did Dickens' experience of childhood poverty affect his life and his writing?" At this point, it is a good idea to talk to your professor and get his or her approval for your topic and research question. Your professor can guide you in developing a question that will lead to a paper of the correct length.

Now you can do research to find the answer to your research question. As you do research, also create a *working bibliography*. A working bibliography is just a rough draft of your Works Cited page, not necessarily in alphabetical order. Whenever you find a source that looks useful, list that source on your working bibliography. This will ensure that you have all the information that you will need later for the final draft of your Works Cited page. Nothing is more frustrating that having to go back to the library the day before your paper is due to try to find a source again because you forgot to write down the city where a book was published, etc. If you record detailed information on your working bibliography while you do your research, writing the final draft of your Works Cited will be a breeze.

Evaluating Sources

Accuracy
When you go to the library and find a book on your topic, you can be fairly sure that the information in that book will be accurate and reliable. The library only buys books that are published by reputable publishing companies.

A reputable publishing company only prints books by authors who are experts in their field, and an editor reads the book carefully to check its accuracy before sending the book to the printer. Most newspapers and magazines have a similar process for ensuring that the information they print is accurate.

The internet has a tremendous amount of information, but you will need to evaluate each site to see if it is reliable. Who created the website? Who wrote the article or entry? If you can't tell, or if the site doesn't give the author's credentials, you should look for a different site. Most professors will not accept information found on Wikipedia because anyone can post information to the site. Wikipedia can be a useful research tool, however, because you can find links to other more reliable sources by going to the bottom of the Wikipedia entry.

Dates
For some research topics, such as climate change, it is important that your information be current. Check the date when the source was written to make sure the information is up-to-date. For other topics, such as Charles Dickens, older sources are fine.

Bias

By reading a variety of sources, you will be able to tell if one of the sources is biased. If several sources give similar interpretations of an event, and another source gives a totally different interpretation, consider why this source is so different. Does the author have special knowledge that makes his/her opinion more valid? Or does the author have a personal bias for or against the issue that makes his/her opinion less valid?

Taking Notes

As you do research and find useful information, you will need to take notes for your paper. Taking notes is an important step of the research process. The time you spend taking careful notes will save you time later when you actually write your paper.

You can write your notes on index cards or notebook paper, or you can type them directly onto the computer. Whichever method you choose, be sure to follow these four guidelines:

o   Each note should be *short*. If you write on index cards, each note will have to be short because you will run out of space on the card. If you write on notebook paper or type on the computer, type a short note and then leave several blank lines on the page before typing the next note.

o Write a *key word* at the top of each note. The key word shows you at a glance what type of information is covered in that note. This will be helpful when it's time to rearrange your notes to create paragraphs in your paper. When Jane took notes on Dickens, her key words included terms like *childhood, marriage, charity, novels, insecurity, show off.*

o Write a *parenthesis* (in-text citation) at the end of each note. This citation should be just like the parentheses you will put in your paper to tell your reader where that information came from. Writing all those parentheses may seem repetitive when you have a page of notes and each note has the same parentheses at its end. But including a parentheses after each note allows you to rearrange the notes later without losing track of which source each note came from. When your paper is nearly finished, it is not fun to have to go through one of your sources again trying to find a bit of information because you forgot to write down the page number when you were taking notes.

o Be careful about *paraphrasing and quoting.* If you paraphrase, be sure to put the information completely in your own words. See page 175 for information about paraphrasing. If you copy word-for-word directly from the source, write quotation marks around the words you copied so you remember that those words came from the source. See page 182 for information on doing quotations.

Example of a note written on an index card:

Charity

Dickens sat in on meetings of Parliament and learned what was going on in English politics. He was concerned that the politicians did not care much about the hardships of the common people. He decided to use his writing to make people aware of the problems that common people faced. He wanted to be "the conscience of the land" (Haines 21).

Example of a note typed onto the computer:

Charity

Dickens sat in on meetings of Parliament and learned what was going on in English politics. He was concerned that the politicians did not care much about the hardships of the common people. He decided to use his writing to make people aware of the problems that common people faced. He wanted to be "the conscience of the land" (Haines 21).

From Notes to Rough Draft

After you have taken your notes, look at the key words at the top of each note (*childhood, marriage, charity, etc.*) and rearrange the notes to put all the similar information together.

- If you took notes on index cards, just rearrange the cards into separate stacks for each key word.

- If you took notes on notebook paper, use scissors to cut the notes apart, and rearrange your slips of paper into stacks.

- If you took notes directly onto the computer, just cut and paste the notes around on the page.

Keep rearranging until you have all your information in the correct order for each paragraph of your paper. You may find that you have similar information from several different sources. Eliminate any notes that you decide you don't need.

If your notes were written by hand, you will now need to type the information onto the computer. Be sure to include all the parentheses!

Now you have the skeleton for your paper on the computer. All the information is in the right order (more or less). A little more work will turn your skeleton into a rough draft, and best of all, your parentheses are already in place. As you work on revising for smoothness and clarity, you can remove parentheses that are not needed. See page 189 for information on where to put parentheses.

Time Saving Tip:

Create your rough draft when you think you are about 75% finished taking notes. If you take all the notes you think you will need, you may have far more information than you can use in your paper. When you create your rough draft, you may find that you don't need to take any more notes. If you do need to take more notes, you will see exactly what kind of information you still need to complete your paper.

Paraphrasing

When you paraphrase, you read something, think about what it means, and rewrite the information in your own words. You do not need to include every detail from the original text. Include the information that you believe is important and leave out the rest, but be careful not to change the meaning of the text.

Read the original text on the next page, and then compare it to the paraphrases below.

Original text from *Tarzan of the Apes* by Edgar Rice Burroughs:

From the time Tarzan left the tribe of great anthropoids in which he had been raised, it was torn by continual strife and discord. Terkoz proved a cruel and capricious king, so that, one by one, many of the older and weaker apes, upon whom he was particularly prone to vent his brutish nature, took their families and sought the quiet and safety of the far interior.

But at last those who remained were driven to desperation by the continued truculence of Terkoz, and it so happened that one of them recalled the parting admonition of Tarzan:

"If you have a chief who is cruel, do not do as the other apes do, and attempt, any one of you, to pit yourself against him alone. But, instead, let two or three or four of you attack him together. Then if you will do this, no chief will dare to be other than he should be, for four of you can kill any chief who may ever be over you."

And the ape who recalled this wise counsel repeated it to several of his fellows, so that when Terkoz returned to the tribe that day he found a warm reception awaiting him.

There were no formalities. As Terkoz reached the group, five huge, hairy beasts sprang upon him.

At heart he was an arrant coward, which is the way with bullies among apes as well as among men, so he did not remain to fight and die, but tore himself away from them as quickly he could and fled into the sheltering boughs of the forest.

Two more attempts he made to rejoin the tribe, but on each occasion he was set upon and driven away. At last he gave it up, and turned, foaming with rage and hatred, into the jungle.

Example of a well-written paraphrase:

The apes did not get along peacefully after Tarzan left. The new king of the apes, Terkoz, was very harsh and mean. Many of the other apes moved farther into the jungle to get away from him. One of the apes who stayed in the community remembered some advice that Tarzan had given before he left. Tarzan had said that the apes should work together to get rid of a bad king. So five apes attacked Terkoz all at once. Terkoz was afraid, so he ran away into the jungle. He tried to come back twice, but the other apes would not let him return.

Example of a badly-written paraphrase:

From the time Tarzan left, the tribe was torn by continual strife. Terkoz was a cruel and capricious king, so many of the older and weaker apes moved to the quiet and safety of another part of the jungle. An ape who remained recalled the advice of Tarzan. Tarzan told them to let two or three or four apes attack a bad king together. So when Terkoz returned to the tribe, five apes sprang upon him. Terkoz was a coward, so he did not fight back, but ran away into the forest. Two more times he tried to return to the tribe, but each time he was attacked and driven away.

Exercise 10.1 Analyzing Paraphrase:

1. Imagine that you are a professor reading the badly-written paraphrase. Even if you had never read the original text, why might you suspect that the student had not paraphrased carefully?

2. Imagine that you are a professor reading the well-written paraphrase. Even if you had never read the original text, why would you believe that the student had paraphrased carefully?

    > Original texts often have a formal, academic style or tone. When you write a paper, your writing should sound like you. How often do most people use the word *capricious*? While it is important to use an appropriate level of formality in a research paper, your writing should be clear and sound natural, not stuffy or artificial. See page 131 for more info about wordiness and choice of language.

3. Look for places where the badly-written paraphrase uses the same words as the original text; this is called plagiarism.

4. How does the well-written paraphrase change those words?

5. Find some places where the well-written paraphrase **does** use the same words as the original text. Why is it necessary to use those exact words?

When you paraphrase, you must change the words that can be changed. What are some different ways you could express the idea of *continual strife*?

Some words in the original text cannot be changed. If the ape king's name is *Terkoz*, you can't call him *Steve* just to use a different word. The same is true for names of places, dates, etc.

6. Look for places where the badly-written paraphrase uses the same sentence structure as the original text.

7. How does the well-written paraphrase use different sentence structures?

Even when the well-written paraphrase uses the same word as the original, the parts of the sentence are rearranged so that the paraphrased sentence is quite different from the original text. If you need to paraphrase information that includes words you can't change, be sure to rearrange the parts of the sentence:

Original text: Charles Dickens was born on February 7, 1812, at Landport, near the city of Portsmouth, England.

Paraphrase: Charles Dickens was born near Portsmouth, England, in 1812.

Writers often include some quotations within their paraphrase. This allows the writer to copy some words from the original that are important in meaning or that express an idea vividly.

Turn to page 182 for an explanation of including quotations in your writing.

Example of a well-written paraphrase which includes quotations:

The apes did not get along peacefully after Tarzan left. The new king of the apes, Terkoz, was "cruel and capricious" (Burroughs 238). Many of the other apes moved farther into the jungle to get away from him. One of the apes who stayed in the community remembered some advice that Tarzan had given them before he left. Tarzan had said that the apes should work together to get rid of a bad king. So five apes attacked Terkoz all at once. Terkoz was "an arrant coward," so he "fled into the sheltering boughs of the forest" (Burroughs 239). He tried to come back twice, but the other apes would not let him return.

Paraphrase vs. Summary:

A summary is just like a paraphrase except that it is much shorter. Here is an example of a well-written summary of the same original text:

Terkoz, the new king, was mean, so some of the apes left the community. Other apes followed Tarzan's advice and cooperated to drive Terkoz away.

Tips for paraphrasing

1. Work on about half of a paragraph at a time. If you try to work in smaller sections, such as one sentence at a time, paraphrasing will be difficult.

2. Some original texts can be difficult to understand. Read slowly and carefully. Look up unfamiliar words. Think how you could explain the information so that your reader can understand it easily.

3. When the information is clear in your mind, write it down in your own words without looking at the original text. Your version will probably be shorter than the original.

4. Finally, compare your paraphrase to the original text. Make sure that the information is the same but the words and sentence structures are different.

5. See page 182 for information on using quotation marks for copying the exact words from the original.

Quotations

Most professors will expect you to include some quotations in a research essay. Quotations add variety to your writing and credibility to your argument. The best way to learn how to use quotations effectively is to analyze a well-written essay.

Exercise 10.2 Analyzing Use of Quotations

Look through the research paper on Charles Dickens on page 162 and find places where the student has quoted words from one of her sources.

1. How many quotations did she use in her essay?

2. How does the number of quotations relate to the number of paragraphs in the essay?

    There is no strict rule about how many quotations should be in a research essay.

    Some paragraphs may not have any quotations, and other paragraphs may have two or more. You want to have a good balance between the number of quotations and the length of your essay. **About one or two quotations per paragraph is a good guideline**, but this is not a rule that you need to follow strictly.

3. How long are the quotations?

    Most of your quotations should be short. Your paper should be mostly your own words (paraphrase). If you want to use a longer quotation—four or more lines of typing—set it off as a block quote by indenting the entire quotation ten spaces. The indentation shows the reader that this is a quotation, so you don't need to use quotation marks. Look at paragraph 4 to see an example of a block quote.

4. Why did the author choose to quote these passages in her essay?

> The author copied words from her sources that she thought were important in meaning or wording. She could have put the information into her own words if she wanted to, but she decided that using the exact words from a source would sound more powerful.

5. Is each quotation smoothly integrated into the sentence?

> Yes, the author's own words flow smoothly into each quotation. Compare the two sentences below, and explain why the first sentence is smooth and the second sentence is not smooth:
>
> He showed off by wearing flashy clothes such as "flamboyantly colored waistcoats."
>
> Dickens was a show off "flamboyantly colored waistcoats."
>
> The second sentence requires the reader to figure out that the flamboyantly colored waistcoats are an example of one way that Dickens was a show off.

6. Where did the author put information from her sources into her own words rather than copying the source and using quotation marks?

> Most of the information in this essay is in the author's own words. This is called paraphrasing. Turn to page 175 for an explanation of paraphrasing.

7. Which quotations include ellipses (...)?

> The quotations in paragraphs 4 and 5 have ellipses (three periods with spaces between them) to show that the author left off some words at the end of the sentence.

8. Find several places where the author obviously left some words off of the quotation but did NOT use ellipses. Why didn't the author use ellipses on those quotations?

> You must use ellipses to show the reader that you left off some words *only* when the reader wouldn't otherwise know it. If your quotation is not a complete sentence, it's obvious that you must have left off words, so you don't need to use ellipses.

> If you leave some words off but your quotation is still a complete sentence, put ellipses where you left off the words, either at the beginning of the quotation, in the middle, or at the end. Of course, be sure that you don't change the meaning of the quotation when you leave off words.

9. Where did the author use square brackets [ ] in a quotation?

> In paragraph 5, the author wanted to explain the meaning of the word *waistcoat*. Any time you need to insert your own words into a quotation, put square brackets around the words you are inserting: [vest].

> What if the source you are quoting from has a mistake, like a misspelling? When you are quoting, you must copy the original source exactly. You can use the Latin word *sic*, which means *thus*, to tell the reader that this mistake was in the original source and you just copied it: "He was a man of great viger [sic] and energy."

Signal Phrases

You can use a signal phrase to introduce a quote or paraphrased information. A signal phrase gives the author's name and any other information that would help provide a context for the quote or give credibility to the source.

> According to Cody, Dickens' miserable experience at the factory "haunted him all of his life."

> Noted Dickens biographer David Cody argues that Dickens' miserable experience at the factory "haunted him all of his life."

Smith calls Dickens "a major philanthropist."

Haines points out that Dickens continued working until his death at age fifty-eight (165–67).

Notice that the verb in each signal phrase is in the present tense: *argues, calls, points out.* Other verbs that are frequently used in signal phrases include *believes, claims, denies, reports, thinks,* and *writes.*

Also, only the quote from Haines ends with a parenthetical note because the book by Haines is the only source for which page numbers need to be given. Since the author's name is given in the signal phrase, there is no need to include it in a parenthetical note.

Some professors prefer that you introduce every quote or paraphrase with a signal phrase; for other professors signal phrases are not as important. If you're unsure about using signal phrases, ask your professor for guidance.

Exercise 10.3 Punctuating Quotations

Correct the mistakes in these quotations. Check your answers on page 264.

Original:

O'Keefe is neither crusty nor eccentric. She is simply hard, a straight shooter, a woman clean of received wisdom and open to what she sees.

Quotation with incorrect punctuation:

When Joan Didion profiled artist Georgia O'Keefe, she noted that "O'Keefe is neither crusty nor eccentric." "She is simply hard, a straight shooter, a woman clean of received wisdom and open to what she sees."

Original:

There are three faithful friends—an old wife, and old dog, and ready money.

Quotation with incorrect punctuation:

"An old wife, an old dog, and ready money, says Franklin, are three faithful friends."

Original:

Keep your eyes wide open before marriage, half shut afterwards.

Quotation with incorrect punctuation:

The counselor quoted Ben Franklin to the couple: Keep your eyes "wide open" before marriage, but keep them "half shut" afterwards.

Original:

The ancient precept "Know Thyself" and the modern precept "Study Nature" become at last one maxim.

Quotation with incorrect punctuation:

Ralph Waldo Emerson writes, "the ancient precept "Know Thyself" and the modern precept "Study Nature" become at last one maxim".

Original:

I never met a man I didn't like.

Quotation with incorrect punctuation:

Will Rogers said, "he never met a man he didn't like".

Parenthetical Notes

When you write a research paper, you must let your reader know your source for each bit of information. Some documentation styles use footnotes or endnotes to do this. The MLA documentation style uses parenthetical notes (also called in-text citations).

Documenting your sources with parenthetical notes can seem confusing, but really it is quite logical. Do the following two exercises to analyze the parentheses in the essay on Dickens, and you will see how parenthetical notes work to show the reader which source each bit of information came from.

Exercise 10.4 Color-Coding of Sources

Turn to page 192 and use colored pencils, markers, or highlighters in four different colors to analyze the documentation used in this research essay.

Step 1. Use your first color to highlight the first source listed on the list of Works Cited: the article written by David Cody.

Step 2. Use that same color to highlight every parenthetical note that has the name Cody.

Step 3. Starting with each parenthesis you have colored for Cody, work backwards and color in the text of the essay until you come to the beginning of the paragraph or a parenthesis with a different name in it.

Now everything in this essay that came from the article by David Cody is highlighted with your first color.

Step 4. Use your second color to highlight the second source listed on the list of Works Cited: the entry about Charles Dickens which was taken from the reference book titled *British Authors.*

Step 5. Use that same color to highlight every parenthetical note that has the name "Dickens."

Step 6. Starting with each parenthesis you have colored for "Dickens," work backwards and color in the text of the essay until you come to the beginning of a paragraph or a parenthesis with a different name in it.

Now everything in this essay that came from the entry about Charles Dickens in the reference book *British Authors* is highlighted with your second color.

Step 7. Use your third color to highlight the third source listed on the list of Works Cited: the book by Charles Haines.

Step 8. Use that same color to highlight every parenthetical note that has the name Haines.

Step 9. Starting with each parenthesis you have colored for Haines, work backwards and color in the text of the essay until you come to the beginning of a paragraph or a parenthesis with a different name in it.

Now everything in this essay that came from the book by Charles Haines is highlighted with your third color.

Step 10. Use your fourth color to highlight the fourth source listed on the list of Works Cited: the article by Kyle Smith.

Step 11. Use that same color to highlight every parenthetical note that has the name Smith.

Step 12. Starting with each parenthesis you have colored for Smith, work backwards and color in the text of the essay until you come to the beginning of a paragraph or a parenthesis with a different name in it.

Now everything in this essay that came from the article by Kyle Smith is highlighted with your fourth color.

Look at the highlighted essay and notice that nearly everything is highlighted one of your four colors.

The sentences that are not highlighted are the author's own thoughts and opinions. As you can see, the parenthetical notes show the reader which information came from each source on the list of Works Cited.

Jane Doe

Professor Jones

English 111

20 April 2013

Charles Dickens

Poverty, Success, and Social Justice

When Charles Dickens was born to a struggling, working-class family in 1812, no one dreamed that he would become a wealthy British novelist and author of classic books including *Oliver Twist*, *Great Expectations*, *A Christmas Carol*, and *David Copperfield* (Cody). Since many of the events and characters in his books were taken from his own life experiences, his poor background shaped his writing as well as his personality.

Dickens' father was a clerk; his mother was of "slightly higher social class" ("Dickens"). His poor but stable family life changed suddenly when he was twelve years old. Dickens' father was sent to London's Marshalsea Prison for Debtors, and Dickens had to quit school and get a job working in a factory (Haines 6–8). His miserable experience at the factory "haunted him all of his life" and left him "scarred psychologically" (Cody).

Then, miraculously, his father received a large inheritance, left prison, and sent Dickens back to school. After finishing school at age fifteen, Dickens held various jobs including clerk for a solicitor (lawyer) and newspaper typist. He began selling stories to magazines and newspapers in 1833. In 1836 a collection of his stories was published as his first book ("Dickens"). He began writing his first novel, *Oliver Twist*, in 1837 (Cody).

In the following years, Dickens wrote many novels and became famous. He used his fame to try to change society by writing about the lives of the poor. Most of his middle and upper class readers had no idea that people were treated so unfairly. In time, Dickens became wealthy, and his used his money to help others:

> He was a major philanthropist who expertly used his name and his time to draw attention to the scandalous condition of the poor. He took pity on children whose education he paid for and anonymously sent money to desperate men and women, including prisoners. . . . (Smith)

At the same time, Dickens' hard childhood made him "insecure emotionally" (Cody). He showed off by wearing expensive, flashy clothes such as "gold chains and rings, and flamboy-antly colored waistcoats [vests]" ("Dickens"). He treated his wife, Catherine, terribly. After she gave birth to their third son, Dickens refused to see the baby, and he criticized Catherine for getting fat. Since divorce was not allowed at that time, they sep-arated, and Dickens said, "That figure is out of my life for ever-more . . ." (qtd. in Smith).

Dickens' health suffered from his busy schedule of writing and promoting his books. After a trip to America, he returned home exhausted, his health "permanently broken" ("Dickens"). He continued writing until he was fifty-eight when he died of a stroke (Haines 165–67).

Dickens' childhood of poverty and humiliation had good and bad effects. While it led him to be insecure and sometimes cruel, it also made him compassionate, "a champion of the op-pressed" ("Dickens"). His descriptions of suffering and injus-tice raised the consciousness of his readers which helped improve life for working people of England.

Works Cited

Cody, David. "Dickens: A Brief Biography." *The Victorian Web: Literature, History, and Culture in the Age of Victoria.* N.p. Mar. 2004. Web. 27 Dec. 2011.

"Dickens, Charles." *British Authors of the Nineteenth Century.* Ed. Stanley J. Kunitz. New York: Wilson, 1936. Print.

Haines, Charles. *Charles Dickens.* New York: Franklin Watts, 1969. Print.

Smith, Kyle. "Humbug!" *New York Post.* Review of *Charles Dickens: A Life* by Claire Tomalin. *NYPost.com.* 24 Dec. 2011. Web. 25 Dec. 2011.

Exercise 10.5 Analyzing Use of Parentheses

Analyze the use of parentheses in the research essay on page 192.

1. Where has the student put a parenthetical note (also called an in-text citation) in her essay?

   > The student put a parenthesis at the end of every sentence that includes a quotation. She also put a parenthesis at the end of each section of paraphrased information. By looking at your highlighted colors, you can see that a parenthesis marks the end of a section of paraphrased information.

2. Find a place where a section of paraphrase is only one sentence long.

   > Sometimes the sections are quite short because the student switched between sources frequently.

3. What is the longest section of paraphrase in the essay?

   > The information in paragraph 4 all came from the article written by Kyle Smith. Since the quotation is at the end of the paragraph, only one parenthesis is needed.

4. Can you find a place where the parenthesis comes in the middle of the sentence?

   > No. Save the parenthesis for the end of the sentence. The only time you would put a parenthesis in the middle of a sentence would be if

the first part of the sentence came from one source
and the second part came from another source:

> Dickens was "insecure emotionally" (Cody),
> so he showed off by wearing "gold chains and
> rings" ("Dickens").

5. Does the period go before or after the parenthesis?

    Notice that the period which ends the sentence
    comes *after* the parenthesis except in the block
    quotation where it comes before the parenthesis.

6. Can you find a parenthesis that contains more than
    just one word?

    At the end of paragraph 5, we see something
    unusual: (qtd. in Smith). The quotation is Charles
    Dickens' own words, not Smith's words. Since the
    author of this essay read Dickens' words in the
    article by Smith, she has cited the quotation to
    Smith.

7. Do any of the parentheses in this essay include page
    numbers?

    Only the parentheses for the book by Charles
    Haines contain page numbers. The student did
    not need to use page numbers for her other
    sources. The two web pages did not have page
    numbers, and *British Authors* is a reference book
    that is arranged alphabetically. If someone wants
    to look up Charles Dickens in an alphabetical ref-
    erence book such as an encyclopedia, he or she

would turn to the D section and never even look at the page numbers.

You should include the page numbers for sources such as books, magazines, newspapers, or web pages that have page numbers. Look carefully at the parentheses for Haines, and you will see that only one blank space comes between the name Haines and the page number. You don't need to use a comma or type *pg.* or *page.*

Page numbers from newspaper articles are usually a letter for the section of the newspaper and then a number for the page in that section. See page 205 for more information about page numbers for newspaper articles.

8. Can you imagine a situation in which you might have a parenthesis with only page numbers and no words?

> Sometimes it works well to introduce your quotation or paraphrase with a signal phrase:

>> According to Haines, Dickens was born in 1812 (3).

> Since the author's name is given in the signal phrase, the parenthesis gives only the page number. See page 185 for more information about signal phrases.

9. Why must you be careful about using signal phrases with a source that does not have any page numbers?

> If you give the author's name in a signal phrase and the source doesn't have page numbers, there is nothing left for you to put in the parentheses. Since you wouldn't need a parenthesis in that spot, your reader may not know where the information from that source ends and the information from the next source begins.

>> According to Cody, Dickens' miserable experience at the factory "haunted him all of his life" and left him "scarred psychologically." Dickens' hard childhood made him "insecure emotionally." He showed off by wearing expensive, flashy clothes such as "gold chains and rings, and flamboyantly colored waistcoats [vests]" ("Dickens").

> Without a parentheses to mark the end of the information from Cody, the reader might not be sure where the information from Cody ends and the information from "Dickens" begins.

> To fix this problem, add a parenthesis at the end of the information from Cody even though his name was given in the signal phrase.

Common Knowledge

You can omit documentation for information that would be considered *common knowledge*. Common knowledge includes information that most readers would certainly know. Here are some examples:

> George Washington was the first president of the United States.

> The Declaration of Independence was signed in Philadelphia, Pennsylvania, on July 4, 1776.

> Plants create their food from sunlight by using a process called photosynthesis.

If you have any doubt about whether information qualifies as common knowledge, be safe and document the information.

List of Works Cited

When you write a research paper, you must include a list of all the sources you used. This list should be a separate page at the end of the paper.

Works Cited

Cody, David. "Dickens: A Brief Biography." *The Victorian Web: Literature, History, and Culture in the Age of Victoria.* N.p. Mar. 2004. Web. 27 Dec. 2011.

"Dickens, Charles." *British Authors of the Nineteenth Century.* Ed. Stanley J. Kunitz. New York: Wilson, 1936. Print.

Haines, Charles. *Charles Dickens.* New York: Franklin Watts, 1969. Print.

Smith, Kyle. "Humbug!" *New York Post.* Review of *Charles Dickens: A Life* by Claire Tomalin. *NYPost.com.* 24 Dec. 2011. Web. 25 Dec. 2011.

Exercise 10.6 Analyzing Works Cited Structure

1. What order are the sources arranged in?

    They are alphabetical.

2. How is the indenting done?

    The first line of each listing is on the left margin,
    and the following lines are indented five spaces. This
    format makes it easy for the reader to look down
    the alphabetical list to find any of the sources.

Citing Sources in Parentheses
and the List of Works Cited

The official handbook for MLA documentation style gives directions and examples of every imaginable type of source you might
need to cite in your research paper. The chapter on creating your
list of Works Cited is ninety pages long. The chapter covering
parenthetical citations is twenty pages long. If you have an unusual situation for one of your sources, you can look it up in the
MLA handbook or on the website owl.english.purdue.edu.

The examples below cover the most common types of sources
and situations that you will encounter in your research.

A Book with One Author
Kauffman, Michael W. *American Brutus: John Wilkes Booth and
    the Lincoln Conspiracies.* New York: Random House, 2004.
    Print.

Parenthesis for this source (Kauffman 68).

A Book with Two Authors

Gies, Frances and Joseph Gies. *Life in a Medieval Village.* New
York: Harper and Row, 1990. Print.

Parenthesis for this source (Gies and Gies 139).

A Book with Three Authors

Okuda, Michael, Denise Okuda, and Debbie Mirek. *The Star
Trek Encyclopedia: A Reference Guide to the Future.* New
York: Pocket, 1994. Print.

Parenthesis for this source (Okuda, Okuda, and Mirek 383).

A Book with an Unknown Author / Book with
More than One Edition

MLA Handbook for Writers of Research Papers. 7th ed. New York:
Modern Language Association, 2009. Print.

Parenthesis for this source (*MLA Handbook* 29).

Since the author's name is not given, put a shortened version of
the title of the book in your parentheses. Be sure to italicize the
title in the parentheses to show that it is the title of a book.

Some books have been published more than once. These books
will say Second Edition, Third Edition, etc. on the cover. Place
this information right after the title of the book in your Works
Cited listing.

A Book with Sections or Chapters Written by Different Authors / Book with an Editor

Sitler, Robert K. "2012 and the Maya World." *The Mystery of 2012: Predictions, Prophecies, and Possibilities.* Ed. Tami Simon. Boulder, CO: SoundsTrue, 2007. 89–107. Print.

Parenthesis for this source (Sitler 101–6).

The author and title for the chapter you used are given first and then the information about the book in which you read that chapter. The page numbers 89–107 are the pages on which this chapter appears in the book. Tami Simon is the editor of this book.

Encyclopedia or Dictionary Entry

"The Dave Matthews Band." *The Definitive Illustrated Encyclopedia of Rock.* 1ˢᵗ Ed. 2007. Print.

Parenthesis for this source ("Dave Matthews").

The words in quotation marks are the words that you looked up in the encyclopedia or dictionary. The author's name was not given for the encyclopedia entry.

A Magazine Article

Shute, Nancy. "If We Only Had Wings." *National Geographic.* Sept. 2011: 67–79. Print.

Parenthesis for this source (Shute 69).

A Newspaper Article

Cave, Damien. "Migrants' New Paths Reshaping Latin America."
New York Times 6 Jan. 2012: A1+. Print.

Parenthesis for this source: (Cave A1).

In newspapers, an article will often begin on one page and then continue on another page. The article cited above started on page A-1 and then skipped ahead to page A-8. The page number is given as A-1+ because the article was not only on page A-1, but it was not on all the pages in between.

A Newspaper Article with an Unknown Author

"African Union Extends Somalia Force." New York Times 6 Jan.
2012: A8. Print.

Parenthesis for this source ("African Union" A8).

Since the author's name is not given, put a shortened version of the title in your parentheses. Put quotation marks around the title so that the reader knows that it is a title.

Editorial in a Newspaper

"Donors, Secrecy and That Loophole." Editorial. New York
Times 6 Jan. 2012: A22. Print.

Parenthesis for this source ("Donors" A22).

Movie Review

Lindsey, Craig. "Office Geopolitics: A Solid Revival of Cold War-era le Carre novel." Rev. of *Tinker Tailor Soldier Spy*. Dir. Tomas Alfredson. *Independent Weekly* 4 Jan. 2012: 28. Print.

Parenthesis for this source (Lindsey 28).

Web Site

Perdue, David. *David Perdue's Charles Dickens Page*. David Perdue, 15 Jan. 2012. Web. 16 Jan. 2012.

Parenthesis for this source: (Perdue).

The name David Perdue which appears after the title of the web site is the name of the publisher of the site. The first date given is the date that the site was last updated. The second date given is the date that you looked at the site.

Short Work from a Web Site

"John Lee Hooker." *Bio. True Story*. A & E Television Networks, 2012. Web. 19 Dec. 2011.

Parenthesis for this source ("John Lee Hooker").

Work from a Database

Tsafnat, Guy, Joseph Copty, and Sally R. Partridge. "RAC: Repository of Antibiotic Resistance Cassettes." *Oxford Journals*. 8 Nov. 2011. *Database: The Journal of Databases and Curation*. Web. 11 Nov. 2011.

Parenthesis for this source: (Tsafnat, Copty, and Partridge).

Documenting Web Sources

Some websites include information about the author, the publisher, the date, etc., while other websites do not include this information. Put the information that you have in your Works Cited listing, and don't worry about the rest.

If no publisher's name is given for a website, write N.p. in the spot where the publisher's name would normally go. If no date is given, write n.d. in the spot where the date would normally go.

Film or Video

The Apartment. Dir. Billy Wilder. Perf. Jack Lemmon, Shirley MacLaine, Fred MacMurray. United Artists, 1960. DVD.

Parenthesis for this source: (*Apartment*).

Billy Wilder is the name of the director. Jack Lemmon, Shirley MacLaine, and Fred MacMurray are the major performers in the movie.

Radio or Television Program

"Legal Scholar: Jim Crow Still Exists in America." *Fresh Air.* Host Terry Gross. Natl. Public Radio, 16 Jan. 2012. *NPR.org.* Web. 2 Feb. 2012.

Parenthesis for this source: ("Legal Scholar").

Fresh Air is the name of the radio show. The first date given is the date on which the show was broadcast. The second date is the day you listened to the show on the website.

Personal Interview

Johnson, Kenneth. Personal interview. 5 Sept. 2011.

Parenthesis for this source (Johnson).

Tricky Situations for Documentation

Two sources by the same author: On your Works Cited page, alphabetize the sources by the title of the book or article. Type the first listing as usual. For the second source by that author, type three hyphens instead of the author's name:

> Dickens, Charles. *Great Expectations*. London: Dent, 1994. Print.

> —. *Oliver Twist*. London: Penguin, 1985. Print.

In your parentheses, after the author's name, give a shortened version of the title:

(Dickens, *Great* 144)
(Dickens, *Oliver* 225)

Exercise 10.7 Works Cited Listings

Write a Works Cited listing and a parenthesis for each of these sources. Check your answers on page 265.

1. The title of the book is *The Professor and the Madman*. It was published by Harper Collins in New York in 1998. The author's name is Simon Winchester. You used a quote on page 88.

2. The title of the book is *Cutting Gardens*. It was published in 1993, in New York, by Simon and Shuster. The book was written by Anne Halpin and Betty Mackey. You used information from pages 58–60.

3. The article is from the January 2012 edition of the magazine *Smithsonian*. It was written by Eric Wagner. The title of the article is "Way of the Wolverine." The article is on pages 13–15. You used information from page 14.

4. This article was in the *New York Times* on Friday, January 6, 2012. The title of the article is "In East Africa, Towns Suffer in Crackdown on Diamonds." This article starts on page A4 and then skips ahead to page A8. You are using a quote taken from page A8. The article was written by John Eligon.

5. This article was in the *New York Times* on Friday, January 6, 2012. The title of the article is "Election Chief will not Resign." The author's name is not given. The entire article is on page A9.

6. This entry was in the print version of the fifth edition of *The Columbia Encyclopedia*. You were looking for information about the Isle of Man. The entry was listed as "Man, Isle of."

7. The name of the web site is *The Victorian Web: Literature, History, and Culture in the Age of Victoria.* The name of the article you used is "Dickens: A Brief Biography." The article was written by David Cody. The publisher of the web site is not given, but it was last updated in March 2004. You looked at the page on December 27, 2011.

Appendix

Types of Verbs

Verbs can be divided into three groups: **action verbs, linking verbs,** and **helping verbs.**

An **ACTION VERB** is a word that tells what somebody does:

> Josh <u>ate</u> corn flakes for breakfast.

Eating is an action, so *ate* is an action verb.

A **LINKING VERB** tells what somebody or something is:

> The roses <u>are</u> pink.

Do the roses have to do anything to be pink? No. They just are pink. So *are* is a linking verb.

All the forms of the verb *to be* are always linking verbs: am, is, are, was, were, will be. A few other words can be action verbs or linking verbs depending on the sentence:

> The rose <u>smelled</u> good.   Linking verb
>
> Tenisha <u>smelled</u> the rose.   Action verb

In the first sentence, the rose didn't do anything. It just has a fragrance that smells good, so *smelled* is a linking verb. In the second sentence, Tenisha bent down over the rose and sniffed to smell the rose. Tenisha performed an action, so in this sentence *smelled* is an action verb.

A **HELPING VERB** works with a main verb to show complicated tenses or times. **Verb phrases** (two or more words working together as the verb) tell when one thing happened in relationship to something else:

> Before the party began, he <u>had drunk</u> the lemonade. (past perfect)
>
> He <u>has drunk</u> three glasses of lemonade already. (present perfect)
>
> He <u>will have drunk</u> all the lemonade before the cookies are served. (future perfect)
>
> When I arrived, he <u>was drinking</u> lemonade. (past progressive)
>
> He <u>is drinking</u> lemonade right now. (present progressive)

He <u>will be drinking</u> lemonade all afternoon. (future progressive)

He <u>had been drinking</u> lemonade all afternoon. (past perfect progressive)

He <u>has been drinking</u> lemonade all afternoon. (present perfect progressive)

He <u>will have been drinking</u> lemonade all afternoon. (future perfect progressive)

In these sentences, we see several different helping verbs being used with the main verbs **drunk** and **drinking**.

Note: An ING word will never be a verb by itself. But it can be part of a verb phrase as long as one or more helping verbs come before it.

Common Helping Verbs

am	is	are	was	were	will	could
be	been	had	has	have	shall	would

Notice that not all of the words in the verb phrase will change when we change the tense.

Yesterday He **had** drunk the lemonade.
Every day He **has** drunk the lemonade.
Tomorrow He **will have** drunk the lemonade.

The helping verb *had* changes when we change the time, but the main verb *drunk* does not change. This can make it tricky to know exactly which words to mark as the entire verb.

So do this: if you are marking verbs and you notice that the word that changes is on the list of helping verbs, look to see if the next word in the sentence is working with the helping verb to make a verb phrase.

Why does this matter? For practical grammar—what you need to know to write correctly—it doesn't matter. Each sentence you write needs a verb, and you can make sure you have a verb by changing the time. Even though not all the words in a complicated verb phrase will change, at least one of them will change and that will indicate the verb.

Transitive and Intransitive Verbs

Verbs can also be classified as **transitive** or **intransitive**. A transitive verb takes a **direct object**, and an intransitive verb does not. Most verbs can be either transitive or intransitive depending on the sentence:

The <u>wind</u> <u>blew</u>.	Intransitive
The <u>wind</u> <u>blew</u> my **hat** off.	Transitive

In the second sentence, we have a direct object *hat*, so the verb *blew* is transitive in that sentence. For an explanation of direct objects, see page 221.

Verbals—Gerunds and Infinitives

A **GERUND** is a word that looks like a verb, but it has ING on the end, and it is not functioning as the verb in the sentence:

> Jill loves dancing.
> *Yesterday* Jill **loved** dancing.
> *Tomorrow* Jill **will love** dancing.

The word that changed is *loves,* so *loves* is the verb. *Dancing* tells what she loves. *Dancing* is a **direct object**. For an explanation of direct objects, see page 221.

Why isn't *loves dancing* a verb phrase? *Loves* is not one of the helping verbs. *Dancing* could be part of a verb phrase if it had a helping verb:

> Jill <u>was dancing</u>.

A gerund can also be the subject of a sentence:

> <u>Dancing is</u> good exercise.

An **INFINITIVE** is the word *to* followed by a verb. An infinitive does not function as the verb in a sentence:

> Jill loves to dance.
> *Yesterday* Jill **loved** to dance.
> *Tomorrow* Jill **will love** to dance.

The word that changed is *loves,* so *loves* is the verb. *To dance* tells what she loves. *To dance* is a **direct object**.

An infinitive can sometimes be the subject of a sentence:

To dance on Broadway is Jill's dream.

Tricky Sentence Structures

In most sentences, the subject will come before the verb. Here are some unusual sentences in which the subject comes after the verb.

An **EXPLETIVE** is a sentence that starts with *there:*

There is a fly in my soup!

Finding the verb is easy: *is.* But if I ask the subject question—"Who or what is a fly in my soup?"—I am liable to answer *there,* and *there* will never be the subject.

In an expletive, the subject will come after the verb. Follow these steps to find the subject:

There is a fly in my soup!

Step 1)   Eliminate the word *there*: Is a fly in my soup!

Step 2)   Rearrange the remaining words: A fly is in my soup!

Step 3)   Ask the subject question, "Who or what is in my soup?" *Fly.*

Step 4)   Mark the verb and subject in the original sentence: There is a fly in my soup!

Here's another example. The verb is *are*. Follow the steps to find the subject.

> There <u>are</u> two cupcakes left.

Step 1)   Eliminate the word *there*: <u>Are</u> two cupcakes left.

Step 2)   Rearrange the remaining words: Two cupcakes <u>are</u> left.

Step 3)   Ask the subject question, "Who or what are left?" *Cupcakes.*

Step 4)   Mark the verb and subject in the original sentence: There <u>are</u> two <u>cupcakes</u> left.

In an **INTERROGATIVE** sentence (a question) the subject will often come in the middle of a verb phrase. Read about verb phrases on page 212 before you try to find the verbs in questions.

> Did Sally eat the last piece of cake?
> How much cake did Sally eat?

To find the verb and subject in a question, you first have to rewrite the question as a regular sentence by rearranging the words. Be sure to use exactly the same words:

> Sally did eat the last piece of cake.
> Sally did eat how much cake.

Now you can use the regular process to find the verb and the subject.

Every day Sally **does eat** the last piece of cake.
Tomorrow Sally **will eat** the last piece of cake.
"Who or what eats the last piece of cake?" *Sally*.

Every day Sally **does eat** how much cake.
Tomorrow Sally **will eat** how much cake.
"Who or what eats how much cake?" *Sally*

Mark the subject and verb in the original sentence:

<u>Did</u> <u>Sally</u> eat the last piece of cake?
How much cake <u>did</u> <u>Sally</u> <u>eat?</u>

An **IMPERATIVE** sentence is a command:

Scott's mom: "Pick up your dirty clothes."

This sentence does not name the person who needs to pick up the clothes because the name is not necessary. When Scott finishes taking a shower and leaves his dirty clothes all over the bathroom floor, he knows who his mom means when she says, "Pick up your dirty clothes." Scott understands that his mom means YOU (him), so we would say that the subject of this sentence is the **understood you.**

Shannon's roommate: "Please turn the music down."

The verb is *turn.* "Who or what should turn the music down?" The name is not given, but Shannon knows who her roommate means because Shannon is the one playing loud music while her roommate is trying to study. Shannon understands that her roommate means YOU (her).

To mark this type of sentence, write the word *you* in parentheses so that you can underline it as the subject:

> (<u>You</u>) <u>Turn</u> the music down.
> (<u>You</u>) <u>Pick up</u> your dirty clothes.

Sometimes a writer will place the subject after the verb in order to create a **DRAMATIC STYLE**. Finding the verb in this type of sentence can be challenging:

> Out of the hole ran the mouse.

You might want to begin by putting parentheses around the prepositional phrase in this sentence. Since the subject and verb will never be part of a prepositional phrase, eliminating those phrases will make the sentence shorter and easier to work with.

> (Out of the hole) ran the mouse.
> *Every day* **runs** the mouse.
> *Tomorrow* **will run** the mouse.

To find the subject, ask the usual question but stop right after you say the verb. Don't read all the way to the end of the sentence.

> "Who or what ran?" *Mouse*
> Out of the hole <u>ran</u> the <u>mouse</u>.

Analyzing sentences like this is mostly a matter of logic. There's really only one word in this sentence that could be a verb: *ran*. There are really only two words that could be the subject: *hole* or *mouse*. The hole can't run, so the subject must be *mouse*.

Why does this matter?

For practical grammar, it doesn't matter. You can write dramatic sentences in your papers without having to underline the subject and verb. Just be sure that your sentence isn't a fragment, comma splice, or run-on.

Clause Patterns

Direct Objects, Indirect Objects, Object Complements, and Subject Complements

When you're looking at clause patterns, take each clause of the sentence separately and disregard any phrases.

First Clause Pattern: S–V

Subject – Verb

> Snakes bite.
> Maria drove to the store.
> Tom and Sue dined and danced at the Ritz.

Second Clause Pattern: S–V–DO

<u>Subject</u> – <u>Verb</u> – **Direct Object**

To identify a **direct object**, say the subject and the verb, then ask, "what?" Direct objects only answer the question "what?" If a word is answering a different question, such as how or where, it is not a direct object.

<u>Snakes</u> bite **people.**
"Snakes bite what?"   **People**

<u>Maria</u> <u>drove</u> her **car** to the store.
"Maria drove what?"   **Car**

<u>Tom</u> and <u>Sue</u> <u>ate</u> **dinner** at the Ritz.
"Tom and Sue ate what?"   **Dinner**

A gerund or an **infinitive** can also serve as a direct object:

<u>Jackie</u> <u>loves</u> **baking** brownies.
"Jackie loves what?"   **Baking**

<u>Mark</u> <u>wants</u> **to win** the trophy.
"Mark wants what?"   **To win**

Third Clause Pattern: S–V–IO–DO

<u>Subject</u> – <u>Verb</u> – Indirect Object – **Direct Object**

The indirect object receives the direct object.

> <u>Steve gave</u> Jackie a new **car** for her birthday.
> "Steve gave what?"   **Car**
> "Who received the car?"   Jackie

> <u>Jackie bought</u> Steve a **tie.**
> "Jackie bought what?"   **Tie**
> "Who received the tie?"   Steve.

> <u>Chris offered</u> Stefan a **ride** in his plane.
> "Chris offered what?" **Ride**
> "Who received the ride?" Stefan

Fourth Clause Pattern: S–V–DO–OC

<u>Subject</u> – <u>Verb</u> – **Direct Object** – *Object Complement*

The object complement is a noun or adjective that modifies the direct object.

> The <u>potion made</u> **Snow White** *sleepy.*
> "The potion made what?"   **Snow White**
> "Word that describes Snow White?"   *Sleepy*

> <u>Love makes</u> a **house** a *home.*
> "Love makes what?"   **House**
> "Word that describes house?"   *Home*

Guinevere <u>found</u> **Hector** *annoying.*
"Guinevere found what?"   **Hector**
"Word that describes Hector?"   *Annoying*

Fifth Clause Pattern: S–LV–SC (PA/PN)

<u>Subject</u> – <u>Linking Verb</u> – SUBJECT COMPLEMENT

The first four clause patterns are for clauses with action verbs. This is the pattern for a clause with a **linking verb**. See page 211 for information about linking verbs.

The subject complement is either a **predicate adjective (PA)** or a **predicate noun (PN).** It modifies the subject. See pages 229 and 233 for an explanation of nouns and adjectives.

<u>I</u> <u>am</u> HUNGRY.
"Word that describes the subject I?"   HUNGRY
"Is HUNGRY a noun or an adjective?"   Adjective.
So this clause is S–LV–SC (PA)

<u>I</u> <u>am</u> a POINT GUARD.
"Word that describes the subject I?" POINT GUARD
"Is POINT GUARD a noun or an adjective?" Noun.
So this clause is S–LV–SC (PN)

The <u>flowers</u> <u>were</u> BEAUTIFUL.
"Word that describes flowers?" BEAUTIFUL.
"Is BEAUTIFUL a noun or an adjective?" Adjective.
So this clause is S–LV–SC (PA)

Relative Clauses

The most common types of clauses are independent and dependent clauses. An **independent clause** has a subject and a verb, and it expresses a complete idea:

> <u>Ty Jenkins</u> <u>averages</u> fifty points a game.
> IC

A **dependent clause** begins with a **subordinating conjunction** that changes the sound of the clause making it sound unfinished:

> Because <u>Ty Jenkins</u> <u>averages</u> fifty points a game . . .
> DC

A **relative clause** begins with a relative word. The relative word takes the place of the subordinating conjunction and sometimes it also replaces the subject.

> <u>Who</u> <u>averages</u> fifty points a game
> RC

In this clause, the verb is *averages. Who* is the relative word. In this sentence it is replacing both the subject and the subordinating conjunction. This clause would be complete if it were asking a question. But as a statement, it does not express a complete idea; consequently, a relative clause functions like a dependent clause. It depends on another clause.

Relative clauses often appear in the middle of another clause:

> <u>Ty Jenkins</u>, *<u>who</u> <u>averages</u> fifty points a game*, <u>is</u> a first round draft choice.

The relative clause gives useful information, but the independent clause could stand alone:

Ty Jenkins is a first round draft choice.

Common Relative Words

who	whose	which
why	where	that

Here's another sentence with a relative clause in the middle of an independent clause:

Sylvester the Cat, *whose determination exceeds his cleverness,* never catches Tweety Bird.

The independent clause is

Sylvester the Cat never catches Tweety Bird.

In the relative clause, the relative word *whose* is replacing the subordinating conjunction

whose determination exceeds his cleverness

Relative clauses can also come after an independent clause:

I returned to the town *where I grew* up.
Kari wondered *why her car's battery was* dead.
Jacob had to decide *which computer was* best.
He chose the computer *that had the most memory.*

For analyzing sentence types, count relative clauses as dependent clauses. If a sentence has an independent clause and a relative clause, it is complex.

For more on sentence types, see Chapter 9 beginning on page 149.

Kinds of Phrases

There are six kinds of phrases: **infinitive, appositive, prepositional, gerund, participial,** and **absolute.**

An **INFINITIVE PHRASE** begins with an **infinitive**: the word *to* followed by a verb. See page 215 for an explanation of infinitives.

> Steve wanted *to go skiing.*
> *To avoid the rain* Jill decided to stay home.

An **APPOSITIVE PHRASE** renames someone. See page 71 for more info on appositives. The following sentence names the woman once as *my sister* and then names her a second time as *the woman on crutches.*

> My sister, *the woman on crutches,* broke her leg skiing.

A **PREPOSITIONAL PHRASE** begins with a **preposition** and ends with a noun or pronoun. A preposition is something a cat can do with a chair. See page 232 for more information on prepositions.

> That painting *of the ocean* is beautiful.
> The gerbil ran *under the bed.*

A **GERUND PHRASE** begins with a **gerund**, a verb form ending with ING that functions as a noun. In the following sentence the gerund *opening* is a noun serving as the subject of the sentence. See page 215 for more information on gerunds.

See page 229 for an explanation of nouns.

> *Opening this door is* so difficult.

A **PARTICIPIAL PHRASE** begins with a **participle**, a verb form ending with ING that functions as an adjective. In the following sentence the participle *wagging* is modifying the noun *dog*. See page 233 for an explanation of adjectives.

> The dog *wagging its tail* is so friendly.

An **ABSOLUTE PHRASE** includes a noun followed by a participle. An absolute phrase is independent from the rest of the sentence.

> *The train having stopped*, we gathered our luggage.

Do you need to know all these different types of phrases?

NO! For punctuation, all phrases are created equal.

Just follow the directions in Chapter 4 regarding introductory material, non-essential elements, etc. It doesn't matter what kind of phrase you're dealing with.

Parts of Speech

There are eight parts of speech: **verb, noun, pronoun, conjunction, preposition, adjective, interjection,** and **adverb.** Look for the parts of speech in this order, and you can use the process of elimination to identify the more difficult parts of speech.

A dictionary will tell you what parts of speech a word can be. Many words can be different parts of speech depending on the job they are doing in a particular sentence.

Verbs

Verbs are very flexible and versatile. A verb may take many different forms to express action or state of being, number, and time.

Floyd **ate** the pizza.	Action
Pizza **is** delicious.	State of being
Jason **eats** pizza for breakfast.	Singular
All the guys **eat** pizza for breakfast.	Plural
Yesterday Sherry **ate** pizza.	Past
Every day Sherry **eats** pizza.	Present
Tomorrow Sherry **will eat** pizza.	Future

To find the verb of a sentence, use the time words—*yesterday, every day, tomorrow*—to change the time of the sentence. The word that changes when you change the time is the verb. Mark verbs with a <u>double underline</u>.

> After he <u>jogged</u> briskly around the park, Mark <u>went</u> to the nearby Starbucks and <u>had</u> a Chai Tea.

For more on verbs, see Chapter 1.

Nouns

A **noun** is a person, place, thing, or idea. The subject of a sentence will often be a noun, but a sentence may have many other nouns too.

When you are analyzing a sentence for parts of speech, first find the verbs. Then look at the rest of the words and ask yourself if

each word is the name of a person, place, thing, or idea. Mark the nouns with N:

> After he <u>jogged</u> briskly around the park, Mark <u>went</u>
>   N   N
>
> to the nearby Starbucks and <u>had</u> a Chai Tea.
>   N   N

Pronouns

A **pronoun** takes the place of a noun. A pronoun may be the subject of a sentence, or it may perform some other job. Mark pronouns as PN:

Pronouns

I	he	she	we	they	it
me	him	her	us	them	you

Note that possessive pronouns (my, mine, his, her, hers, your, our, their, etc.) function as adjectives. See page 233.

After he <u>jogged</u> briskly around the park, Mark <u>went</u>
   PN   N   N

to the nearby Starbucks and <u>had</u> a Chai Tea.
           N   N

Conjunctions

There are two kinds of conjunctions: **coordinating conjunctions** and **subordinating conjunctions.**

Coordinating Conjunctions

For   And   Nor   But   Or   Yet   So

There are only seven **coordinating conjunctions**, and they are all short words, only two or three letters long. You can use the acronym FANBOYS to remember them.

Mark coordinating conjunctions CC.

Common Subordinating Conjunctions

after	although	as	because
before	if	since	so that
that	though	till	until
unless	when	where	while

A **subordinating conjunction** is the first word of a clause, and it makes the clause dependent.

> Francesca <u>makes</u> her own jewelry.

This is a clause because it has a subject and a verb. It is an independent clause because it expresses a complete idea. If you put a subordinating conjunction at the beginning of the clause, the clause will become dependent:

> *Because* <u>Francesca</u> <u>makes</u> her own jewelry . . . WHAT?

Now this clause sounds unfinished. The subordinating conjunction *because* changed the sound of a clause and made the clause dependent.

Some of the words on the list of subordinating conjunctions can also do other jobs. If the word is truly a subordinating conjunction, it will come at the beginning of a clause and make the clause dependent.

See page 156 for false subordinating conjunctions.

Mark subordinating conjunctions with a wavy underline.

> <u>After</u> he <u>jogged</u> briskly around the park, Mark <u>went</u>
> SC   PN   N   N
>
> to the nearby Starbucks and <u>had</u> a Chai Tea.
>   N   CC   N

Interjections

Interjections are rare, but they are very easy to find. An interjection is a word such as *Oh, Wow, No, Yes,* or *Gosh.* An interjection would be the first word of a sentence. Mark interjections as I.

Gosh, I <u>love</u> grammar!
I   PN   N

See page 63 for information on using commas with interjections.

Prepositions

A **preposition** tells what a cat can do with a chair.

A cat can be	**in** the chair
	under the chair
	beside the chair
	near the chair
	by the chair
	with the chair
A cat can jump	**over** the chair
	on the chair
	into the chair
	off the chair
	from the chair
A cat can run	**around** the chair
	to the chair
	through the legs of the chair
A cat can be so still that it looks like part	**of** the chair

Other prepositions include **about, along, at, beyond, beneath, between, for, like,** and more. You can look in a dictionary to see if a word can be a preposition.

A **prepositional phrase** begins with a preposition and then has another word or two or three to finish the idea. The last word of the prepositional phrase is always a noun or pronoun that is called the **object of the preposition.** Mark prepositions as PR and put parentheses around the entire prepositional phrase.

> After he jogged briskly (around the park), Mark
> SC   PN   PR   N   N
>
> went (to the nearby Starbucks) and had a Chai Tea.
> PR   N   CC   N

Adjectives

An **adjective** is a word that modifies or describes a noun. Adjectives answer the questions "How many? What kind? Which one?" In English, the adjective comes before the noun it describes. Mark adjectives ADJ.

Three special adjectives are the words *a, an,* and *the.* These are called **articles,** and they are always adjectives.

> After he jogged briskly (around the park,)Mark
> SC   PN   PR   ADJ   N   N
>
> went (to the nearby Starbucks) and had a Chai
> PR ADJ   ADJ   N   CC   ADJ ADJ
>
> Tea.
> N

The and *a* are articles, so those are automatically adjectives. *Nearby* answers "Which one?" about the Starbucks. *Chai* answers "What kind?" about the tea.

Another type of word that is always an adjective is a **possessive noun or pronoun**; it answers the adjective question "Which one?"

> That is *Susan's* purse.
> That is *her* purse.

Susan owns the purse. The word *Susan's* seems as if it would be a noun because it is her name. But her name is *Susan*, not *Susan's*. In the second sentence, *her* is a possessive pronoun also telling "Which one?" about the purse.

Possessive Pronouns

my	your	their	her	his
mine	yours	theirs	hers	its

Adverbs

Adverbs are the hardest part of speech to find. That is why we save them for last. When you have found the first seven parts of speech, any words left over are probably adverbs.

Mark adverbs as ADV.

Adverbs answer the questions "How? When? How much?" Adverbs can modify or describe verbs, adjectives, and other adverbs. First let's look at adverbs modifying verbs:

Bill <u>ate</u> quickly.
  N   ADV

Quickly answers "how?" about the verb *ate.*

Bill <u>ate</u> most (of his dinner).
  N   ADV PR ADJ N

Most answers "how much?" about the verb *ate.*

Bill <u>jumped</u> high.
  N   ADV

High answers "how much?" about the verb *jumped.*

Yesterday, Bill broke his arm.
  ADV   N   ADJ N

Yesterday answers "when?" about the verb *broke.*

Bill <u>left</u> the party early.
  N   ADJ   N   ADV

Early answers "when?" about the verb *left.*

The word *not* is also an adverb that modifies a verb. *Not* will often come in the middle of a verb phrase, but it isn't a verb. It's an adverb. *Not* negates the verb.

Bill <u>did</u> not brush his teeth.
  N   ADV   ADJ N

Not negates the verb *did brush*

Adverbs can also modify or describe adjectives.

Bill <u>has</u> a light blue jacket.
  N   ADJ ADV ADJ   N

It is very tempting to mark *light* as an adjective that describes the jacket, but really *light* is answering "what kind?" about the adjective *blue.* Because *light* is modifying *blue,* and *blue* is an adjective, *light* must be an adverb. Don't let this mess you up with the article words, though *(a, an, the).* Articles are always adjectives.

> Bill <u>has</u> a very old car.
>   N   ADJ ADV ADJ N
>
> *Very* is answering "how much?" about the adjective *old.*
> *Old* describes the car, and *very* describes *old.*

Last but not least, an **adverb** can modify or describe another adverb.

> Bill <u>runs</u>   very quickly.
>   N   ADV   ADV
>
> *Quickly* answers "how?" about the verb *runs.*
> *Very* answers "how much?" about the adverb *quickly.*

In the next sentence, *briskly* answers "how?" about the verb *jogged:*

> <u>Afte</u>r he <u>jogged</u> briskly (around the park),
> SC   PN   ADV   PR ADJ N
>
> Mark <u>went</u> (to the nearby Starbucks) and
>   N   PR ADJ   ADJ   N   CC
>
> <u>had</u> a Chai Tea.
> ADJ ADJ N

Answers

Exercise 1.1 Finding Verbs

1. My neighbor George <u>loves</u> gardening.
    Tomorrow My neighbor George <u>will love</u> gardening.
2. Every weekend he <u>works</u> in his yard.
    Tomorrow Every weekend he <u>will work</u> in his yard.
3. George <u>went</u> on-line and <u>ordered</u> six apple trees.
    Every day George <u>goes</u> on-line and <u>orders</u> six apple trees.
4. The trees <u>came</u> in the mail in a large cardboard box; they <u>were</u> only three feet tall.
    Every day The trees <u>come</u> in the mail in a large cardboard box; *every day* they <u>are</u> only three feet tall.
5. George <u>sweated</u> profusely as he <u>dug</u> six holes in his yard.
    Every day George <u>sweats</u> profusely as he <u>digs</u> six holes in his yard.
6. Blisters <u>stung</u> his hands, yet he <u>continued</u> working.
    Every day Blisters <u>sting</u> his hands, yet he <u>continues</u> working.
7. Then he <u>shoveled</u> compost into each hole.
    Every day Then he <u>shovels</u> compost into each hole.
8. After planting the trees, George <u>firmed</u> the soil around their roots.
    Every day After planting the trees, George <u>firms</u> the soil around their roots.

9. Soon the little trees <u>will bloom</u>, and the blossoms <u>will look</u> so pretty.

   Yesterday Soon the little trees <u>bloomed</u>, and *yesterday* the blossoms <u>looked</u> so pretty.

10. In only four years, George <u>will harvest</u> his first apples.

    Yesterday In only four years, George <u>harvested</u> his first apples.

Exercise 1.2 Finding Verbs

1. Video games <u>are</u> a multi-billion-dollar industry.

   Yesterday Video games <u>were</u> now a multi-billion-dollar industry.

2. Many people <u>think</u> that *Pong* <u>was</u> the first video game.

   Yesterday Many people <u>thought</u> that *Pong* <u>was</u> the first video game.

3. *Pong* <u>comes</u> from the game of table tennis; in *Pong* players <u>slide</u> the paddles back and forth to hit the ball.

   Yesterday Pong <u>came</u> from the game of table tennis; in *Pong* players <u>slid</u> the paddles back and forth to hit the ball.

4. Although *Pong* <u>was</u> not the first video game, its success <u>took</u> the video game industry mainstream.

   Every day Although *Pong* <u>is</u> not the first video game, its success <u>takes</u> the video game industry mainstream.

5. Earlier video games <u>included</u> *Spacewar* and *Chase; Chase* <u>was</u> first video game for television.

   Tomorrow Earlier video games <u>will include</u> *Spacewar* and *Chase; tomorrow Chase* <u>will be</u> first video game for television.

6. Some teachers even <u>use</u> computer games to teach their students.

   Yesterday Some teachers even <u>used</u> computer games to teach their students.

7. Programs <u>allow</u> students to play a game after they <u>master</u> a new concept.

   Yesterday Programs <u>allowed</u> students to play a game *yesterday* after they <u>mastered</u> a new concept.

8. Typing programs often <u>include</u> games to improve typing speed.
   Yesterday Typing programs often <u>included</u> games to improve typing speed.

9. Even some museums <u>use</u> video games as part of their displays such as the stock trading simulation game at the Chicago Board of Trade Museum.
   Yesterday Even some museums <u>used</u> video games as part of their displays such as the stock trading simulation game at the Chicago Board of Trade Museum.

10. After finishing these sentences, you <u>will reward</u> yourself and <u>play</u> your favorite video game.
    Yesterday After finishing these sentences, *yesterday* you <u>rewarded</u> yourself and <u>played</u> your favorite video game.

Exercise 1.3 Finding Subjects

1. Professor Smith's literature <u>class</u> <u>will study</u> poetry.
   Yesterday Professor Smith's literature <u>class</u> <u>studied</u> poetry.

2. The <u>registrar</u> <u>spent</u> two days fixing the schedules after the college's computer <u>system</u> <u>crashed</u>.
   Every day The <u>registrar</u> <u>spends</u> two days fixing the schedules after the college's computer <u>system</u> <u>crashes</u>.

3. <u>England</u> <u>established</u> the first toll roads in 1269.
   Tomorrow <u>England</u> <u>will establish</u> the first toll roads in 1269.

4. Dylan's favorite breakfast food <u>is</u> cold pizza.
   Yesterday Dylan's favorite breakfast food <u>was</u> cold pizza.

5. <u>Consumers</u> in the United States <u>discard</u> nearly one hundred million cell phones annually.
   Yesterday <u>Consumers</u> in the United States <u>discarded</u> nearly one hundred million cell phones annually.

6. <u>Tiffany</u> and <u>Erika</u> <u>will work</u> at Burger King this summer; <u>Jasmine</u> <u>will serve</u> as a camp counsellor.
   Every day <u>Tiffany</u> and <u>Erika</u> <u>work</u> at Burger King this summer; *every day* <u>Jasmine</u> <u>serves</u> as a camp counselor.

7. <u>Sharing</u> an apartment <u>requires</u> compromise.
   Yesterday <u>Sharing</u> an apartment <u>required</u> compromise.
   (An apartment by itself doesn't require compromise; sharing requires compromise.)
8. Many <u>people</u> <u>use</u> the internet to reserve hotel rooms.
   Yesterday Many <u>people</u> <u>used</u> the internet to reserve hotel rooms.
9. <u>Germany</u> and <u>Japan</u> <u>recycle</u> more than eighty percent of the glass and paper used in their countries.
   Tomorrow <u>Germany</u> and <u>Japan</u> <u>will recycle</u> more than eighty percent of the glass and paper used in their countries.

Exercise 1.4 Finding Subjects

1. <u>Jeremy</u> <u>bought</u> a new phone last week.
   Every day <u>Jeremy</u> <u>buys</u> a new phone last week.
2. His old <u>phone</u> always <u>dropped</u> calls.
   Every day His old <u>phone</u> always <u>drops</u> calls.
3. <u>Melissa</u> and <u>Kari</u> <u>made</u> an inexpensive desk out of a wooden door and two small file cabinets.
   Every day <u>Melissa</u> and <u>Kari</u> <u>make</u> an inexpensive desk out of a wooden door and two small file cabinets.
4. <u>Friction</u> between the brake pads and the wheel rims on a bicycle <u>creates</u> a bicycle's braking action.
   Yesterday <u>Friction</u> between the brake pads and the wheel rims on a bicycle <u>created</u> a bicycle's braking action.
5. On the day before Christmas, <u>tape, scissors,</u> and wrapping <u>paper</u> <u>cluttered</u> the dining room table.
   Tomorrow On the day before Christmas, <u>tape, scissors,</u> and wrapping <u>paper</u> <u>will clutter</u> the dining room table.
6. <u>Alonzo</u> first <u>finished</u> his calculus homework, and then <u>he</u> <u>started</u> his research paper on Napoleon.
   Tomorrow <u>Alonzo</u> first <u>will finish</u> his calculus homework, and then *tomorrow* <u>he</u> <u>will start</u> his research paper on Napoleon.

7. In the 1960's <u>Eartha Kitt</u> and <u>Cesar Romero</u> <u>made</u> guest appearances on the *Batman* television series.
    Every day In the 1960's <u>Eartha Kitt</u> and <u>Cesar Romero</u> <u>make</u> guest appearances on the *Batman* television series.
8. <u>Chandra</u> and <u>Francis</u> <u>planned</u> to go shopping, but their car's <u>battery</u> <u>was</u> dead.
    Every day <u>Chandra</u> and <u>Francis</u> <u>plan</u> to go shopping, but their car's <u>battery</u> <u>is</u> dead.
9. After his <u>computer</u> <u>crashed</u>, <u>Joseph</u> <u>tried</u> writing his paper by hand.
    Tomorrow After his <u>computer</u> <u>crashes</u>, <u>Joseph</u> <u>will try</u> writing his paper by hand.
10. When <u>he</u> <u>got</u> a cramp in his hand, <u>Joseph</u> <u>went</u> next door and <u>borrowed</u> his neighbor's laptop.
    Tomorrow After <u>he</u> <u>gets</u> a cramp in his hand, *tomorrow* <u>Joseph</u> <u>will</u> <u>go</u> next door and <u>borrow</u> his neighbor's laptop.

Exercise 2.1 Identifying Clauses and Phrases

1.	The bog <u>turtle</u> <u>is</u> the size of your palm	**C**
2.	<u>Lives</u> in the soggy soil of wetlands	**Ph**
3.	The Alabama beach mouse	**Ph**
4.	<u>Makes</u> its home in grassy sand dunes	**Ph**
5.	<u>Construction</u> <u>threatens</u> its habitat	**C**
6.	Snow <u>monkeys</u> <u>are</u> native to Japan	**C**
7.	<u>Live</u> farther north than any other monkey	**Ph**
8.	Thick, soft fur for warmth	**Ph**
9.	Snow <u>monkeys</u> <u>bathe</u> in the steaming water	**C**
10.	Of Japan's natural hot springs	**Ph**

Exercise 2.2 Identifying Prepositional Phrases

1. <u>Josie</u> <u>got</u> lost (in the old building.)
2. The chess <u>club</u> <u>will meet</u> tomorrow (in the library.)

3. <u>Max</u> <u>opened</u> the heavy door, <u>walked</u> (down the hall,) <u>went</u> (into the Registrar's office,) <u>sat</u> (in a chair,) and <u>waited</u> his turn.
4. The <u>mouse</u> <u>dashed</u> out (of the cat's paws) and <u>escaped</u> (into the woods.)
5. <u>Carrie</u> <u>placed</u> her Hannah Montana CD collection (in the trunk) (in the attic) where <u>she</u> <u>kept</u> mementos (from her childhood.)
6. The <u>archeologist</u> <u>found</u> two vases (of pure silver) (beneath a heap) (of rubble.)
7. <u>Renee</u> <u>took</u> some yogurt out (of the refrigerator,) <u>checked</u> the expiration date, and <u>dropped</u> the yogurt (into the trash can.)
8. When the <u>phone</u> (in the classroom) <u>rang</u>, the <u>students</u> sitting (by the teacher's desk) <u>jumped</u> (in their seats.)
9. The <u>Lamborghini</u> <u>sped</u> (around the curves) coming dangerously close (to the edge) (of the cliff.)
10. <u>Rene Descartes</u>, a mathematician (with considerable talent,) <u>invented</u> a branch (of mathematics) known (as analytical geometry.)

Exercise 2.3 Identifying Phrases, Independent Clauses, and Dependent Clauses

1.	Always <u>bite</u> me	**Ph**
2.	I <u>try</u> to kill them	**IC**
3.	When <u>I</u> <u>am</u> outside	**DC**
4.	<u>Drive</u> me crazy	**Ph**
5.	While <u>I</u> <u>mow</u> the grass	**DC**
6.	I <u>can't swat</u> them	**IC**
7.	Because <u>I</u> <u>have</u> to push the mower	**DC**
8.	Before <u>I</u> <u>go</u> outside	**DC**
9.	I <u>put</u> on bug repellent spray	**IC**
10.	To keep the mosquitos away	**Ph**

Exercise 2.4 Identifying Phrases, Independent Clauses, and Dependent Clauses

1.	In the fifteenth and early sixteenth centuries	**Ph**
2.	Since the Aztec society had a strict class structure	**DC**
3.	At the top level of society	**Ph**
4.	The nobles were all related to the emperor	**IC**
5.	Although the nobles performed different jobs	**DC**
6.	Such as judge, priest, or soldier	**Ph**
7.	Middle class people were called commoners	**IC**
8.	Worked as farmers, merchants, and craftsmen	**Ph**
9.	Slaves performed the hardest labor	**IC**
10.	Since they were at the bottom of the social structure	**DC**

Exercise 2.5 Identifying Phrases, Independent Clauses, and Dependent Clauses

1.	The new phone was too complicated	**IC**
2.	For Johnna's mom to use	**Ph**
3.	She gave the phone to Johnna	**IC**
4.	When the phone bill came	**DC**
5.	The bill was extremely high	**IC**
6.	Because Johnna sent too many texts	**DC**
7.	On the bus, during lunch, and even in class	**Ph**
8.	To pay her mom back	**Ph**
9.	Johnna found a job	**IC**
10.	At the cell phone kiosk in the mall	**Ph**

Exercise 2.6 Identifying the Invisible THAT

1. For Valentine's day, Xavier knew that Gwendolyn wanted roses.
2. But he was so broke that he gave her freshly picked dandelions instead.
3. Gwendolyn was so disappointed that she began to cry.
4. Xavier thought that they were tears of joy that she shed.
5. Gwendolyn wished that Xavier was a little more romantic.

Exercise 3.1 Identifying Fragments

1. <u>Weighs</u> more than one hundred pounds.   **F**
2. <u>Since</u> its <u>teeth grow</u> continuously.   **F**
3. The <u>capybara chews</u> on tough grasses.   **OK**
4. To keep its teeth short.   **F**
5. <u>They live</u> near rivers, lakes, and swamps.   **OK**
6. In Central and South America.   **F**
7. <u>Capybaras are</u> excellent swimmers.   **OK**
8. <u>Because they have</u> webbing between their toes.   **F**
9. <u>When they are</u> alarmed.   **F**
10. <u>They make</u> a noise similar to a dog's bark.   **OK**

Exercise 3.2 Identifying Fragments

1. <u>Earthworms live</u> in all parts of the world.   **OK**
2. Except in the arctic and extremely arid regions.   **F**
3. <u>Although worms</u> in the tropics <u>grow</u> up to ten or eleven feet long.   **F**
4. Most <u>earthworms are</u> shorter.   **OK**
5. Usually one to two inches in length.   **F**
6. An <u>earthworm is</u> typically gray or reddish brown in color.   **OK**
7. Five tiny <u>hearts pump</u> the worm's blood.   **OK**
8. <u>Because earthworms are</u> responsible for aerating and mixing the soil.   **F**
9. <u>Earthworms are</u> vital to agriculture.   **OK**
10. <u>As Charles Darwin discovered after he studied</u> them.   **F**

Exercise 3.3 Identifying Fragments

1. The <u>1960's marked</u> the beginning of Rock and Roll.   **OK**
2. <u>When</u> the <u>Beatles came</u> to America in 1964.   **F**
3. Next, the <u>Rolling Stones arrived</u>.   **OK**
4. <u>Mick Jagger was</u> the lead singer.   **OK**

5. In February of 1965.	**F**
6. <u>The Who</u> <u>made</u> the charts in the U.K.	**OK**
7. After <u>they</u> <u>recorded</u> the hit song "I Can't Explain."	**F**
8. In 1966 the Animals' <u>"See See Rider"</u> <u>became</u> a big hit in the U.S.	**OK**
9. In the late sixties.	**F**
10. <u>John Lennon</u> <u>left</u> his wife for Yoko Ono.	**OK**

Exercise 3.4 Fixing Fragments

Bold type indicates the fragments which are now fixed. Where I have fixed #3 by taking out the subordinating conjunction, you could also fix it by taking out a period.

1. <u>Alex</u>, an African gray parrot, <u>was</u> thirty-one when <u>he</u> <u>died</u>. For thirty out of his thirty-one years, <u>he</u> <u>lived</u> in a research lab **at Brandeis University**.
2. Scientist <u>Irene Pepperberg</u> <u>taught</u> him to speak. <u>Pepperberg</u> <u>believed</u> **that** **<u>animals</u> <u>had</u> higher-order thinking capabilities.**
3. **<u>Pepperberg</u> <u>showed</u> him two objects such as a green key and a green cup.** <u>Alex</u> <u>could</u> identify the similarity by saying "color." **To show the difference between the two items**, <u>he</u> <u>spoke</u> the word "shape."
4. <u>Alex</u> also <u>counted</u> and <u>did</u> simple arithmetic. **When <u>Alex</u> <u>died</u> in 2007**, <u>he</u> <u>had</u> finally mastered saying the number seven.
5. Alex's <u>accomplishments</u> <u>seem</u> incredible **because a parrot's <u>brain</u> <u>is</u> approximately the size of a walnut.** <u>Irene Pepperberg</u> <u>demonstrated</u> that <u>animals</u> <u>are</u> capable of higher-level thinking.

Exercise 3.5 Fixing Fragments

Bold type indicates the fragments which are now fixed.

1. <u>Gold</u> <u>has</u> always fascinated humans **because <u>it</u> <u>is</u> beautiful.** As early as 3000 B.C.E., gold <u>crafters</u> in Mesopotamia <u>used</u> gold to create jewelry.
2. <u>Gold</u> <u>is</u> a soft metal **usually combined with other metals including copper or silver.** Throughout history, only about

160,000 <u>tons</u> of gold <u>have been</u> mined, **enough to fill two Olympic-sized swimming pools**.

3. <u>Isaac Newton</u>, once England's Master of the Mint, first <u>created</u> a standard price for gold. **<u>Although</u> most <u>countries</u> <u>stopped</u> tying their currency to the gold standard long ago,** the <u>United States</u> <u>maintained</u> its gold standard until 1971.

4. <u>Gold</u> <u>is</u> usually found with other metals **such as mercury**. **After burning off the mercury,** <u>miners</u> <u>sell</u> the pure gold. **When** <u>miners</u> <u>find</u> gold mixed with copper, <u>they</u> <u>ship</u> it overseas to smelters **for separating the gold from the copper**.

5. **<u>Although</u> <u>humans</u> still <u>want</u> gold,** <u>finding</u> and <u>mining</u> new gold <u>has</u> become more difficult **costing more and causing more damage to the environment**.

Exercise 3.6 Fixing Comma Splices and Run-ons

1. <u>Dinosaurs</u> <u>are</u> classified as reptiles **because** <u>they</u> <u>were</u> cold blooded. (F)
   <u>Dinosaurs</u> <u>are</u> classified as reptiles; <u>they</u> <u>were</u> cold blooded. (A)

2. **While** carnivorous <u>dinosaurs</u> typically <u>had</u> pointy teeth, an herbivore's <u>teeth</u> <u>were</u> flat. (E)
   Carnivorous <u>dinosaurs</u> typically <u>had</u> pointy teeth, **but** an herbivore's <u>teeth</u> <u>were</u> flat. (C)

3. <u>Dinosaurs</u> <u>laid</u> eggs; **however**, most <u>mothers</u> <u>abandoned</u> their nests. (B)
   <u>Dinosaurs</u> <u>laid</u> eggs, **but** most <u>mothers</u> abandoned their nests. (C)

4. Recently discovered <u>dinosaurs</u> <u>include</u> many with unusual features. <u>Scientists</u> <u>are</u> trying to figure out the purpose of those features. (D)
   Recently discovered <u>dinosaurs</u> <u>include</u> many with unusual features; <u>scientists</u> <u>are</u> trying to figure out the purpose of those features. (A)

5. <u>Digging</u> up dinosaur bones <u>is</u> only the beginning for paleontologists; the real <u>challenge</u> <u>is</u> assembling the skeleton.(A)

Digging up dinosaur bones is only the beginning for paleontologists **because** the real challenge is assembling the skeleton. (F)
Digging up dinosaur bones is only the beginning for paleontologists. The real challenge is assembling the skeleton. (D)

Exercise 3.7 Fixing Comma Splices and Run-ons

1. Franklin was born in 1706; he had sixteen brothers and sisters. (A)
   Franklin was born in 1706, and he had sixteen brothers and sisters. (C)
2. Franklin wanted to be a writer, so he worked in his brother's printing shop. (C)
   Since Franklin wanted to be a writer, he worked in his brother's printing shop. (E)
3. He was born in Boston, but Franklin moved to Philadelphia. (C)
   Although he was born in Boston, Franklin moved to Philadelphia. (E)
4. In Philadelphia Franklin met and fell in love with Deborah; consequently, they got married. (B)
   In Philadelphia Franklin met and fell in love with Deborah. They got married. (D)
5. He started a newspaper; it was called *The Pennsylvania Gazette.* (A)
   He started a newspaper, and it was called *The Pennsylvania Gazette.* (C)
6. Because the paper was successful, Franklin became famous. (E)
   The paper was successful; therefore, Franklin became famous. (B)
7. Franklin was also an inventor; he invented the wood stove. (A)
   Franklin was also an inventor, and he invented the wood stove. (C)
8. He discovered that lightning is electricity; consequently, he invented the lightning rod. (B)
   He discovered that lightning is electricity, and he invented the lightning rod. (C)
9. Franklin traveled to England; he advocated for better treatment of the American colonies. (A)

Franklin traveled to England where he advocated for better treatment of the American colonies. (F)

10. Later he signed the Declaration of Independence; he also signed the U.S. Constitution. (A)

Later he signed the Declaration of Independence. He also signed the U.S. Constitution. (D)

Exercise 4.1 Basic Commas

1. First <u>we</u> <u>unloaded</u> all the gear from our cars, and then <u>we</u> <u>set up</u> our tents and gathered firewood. *(Job #2)*

2. <u>Since</u> <u>we</u> <u>didn't</u> have a shower, <u>we</u> <u>washed</u> in the river. *(Job #4)*

3. For dinner <u>we</u> <u>caught</u> some catfish in the river and <u>fried</u> them over the fire. *(None—This is just one clause because there is only one subject.)*

4. <u>Fireflies, crickets</u>, and <u>frogs</u> <u>entertained</u> us <u>as</u> <u>we</u> <u>sat</u> around a campfire and <u>swatted</u> the mosquitoes away. *(Job #1)*

5. <u>We</u> <u>unpacked</u> the marshmallows, chocolate bars, and graham crackers and <u>made</u> smores. *(Job #1)*

6. <u>After</u> our <u>hands</u> and <u>mouths</u> <u>were</u> thoroughly sticky, <u>people</u> <u>began</u> to head toward their tents to sleep. *(Job #4)*

7. <u>Everyone</u> <u>was</u> bedded down and sleeping soundly <u>when</u> <u>rain</u> <u>began</u> to fall. *(No comma is needed since the dependent clause comes after the independent clause.)*

8. One minute the <u>rain</u> <u>fell</u> in a drizzle, and the next minute <u>we</u> <u>were</u> caught in a torrential downpour. *(Job #2)*

9. <u>After</u> the <u>wind</u> <u>knocked</u> one tent over, <u>everyone</u> <u>started</u> to reconsider the wisdom of camping. *(Job #4)*

10. Around 2 a.m. <u>we</u> <u>decided</u> to pack up our tents and drive to Missoula, Montana, to stay in the Motel 6. *(Job #3)*

Exercise 4.2 Basic Commas

1. On May 15, 2012, <u>we</u> <u>came</u> home from the grocery store to find <u>that</u> our pet <u>gerbil</u> <u>had</u> escaped from his cage. *(Job #3)*
2. <u>Leo</u> <u>had</u> chewed a hole in his cage, so <u>we</u> <u>closed</u> the front door to keep him from running outside. *(Job #2)*
3. <u>Since</u> <u>we</u> <u>couldn</u>'t open the door, <u>we</u> <u>passed</u> the grocery bags in through an open window. *(Job #4)*
4. As soon <u>as</u> <u>we</u> <u>put</u> the groceries away, <u>we</u> <u>started</u> looking for Leo. *(Job #4)*
5. <u>We</u> <u>looked</u> under the couch, behind the dresser, and even in the bathtub. *(Job #1)*
6. <u>We</u> even <u>looked</u> under all the dirty clothes on my brother's bedroom floor. *(None)*
7. <u>We</u> <u>didn</u>'t find Leo, but <u>we</u> <u>found</u> three quarters, a marble, and a stale granola bar. *(Job #1)*
8. After several hours of searching, <u>we</u> <u>gave</u> up. *(Job #4)*
9. Before going to sleep, <u>we</u> <u>rigged</u> up a gerbil trap and <u>filled</u> it with sunflower seeds. *(Job #4)*
10. <u>We</u> <u>woke</u> up on May 16, 2012, to find Leo sleeping in the trap, and that same day <u>we</u> <u>bought</u> him a stronger cage. *(Job #3 and #2)*

Exercise 4.3 Advanced Commas

1. The noisy, excited kids crowded into the movie theater. *(Job #6)*
   *The adjectives **noisy** and **excited** are coordinate.*
2. That old blue car is good enough for driving to work. *(None)*
   *The adjectives **old** and **blue** are not coordinate.*
3. My mother, the lady in the pink suit, is the keynote speaker. *(Job #7)*
   *The words **the lady in the pink suit** are not necessary.*
4. People who live in glass houses shouldn't throw stones. *(None)*
   *The words **who live in glass houses** are needed in this sentence.*
5. Football players, therefore, spend a great deal of time in the weight room. *(Job #5)*

6. Dogs that bark all night long drive me crazy. *(None)*
   *The words **that bark all night long** are needed in this sentence.*

7. Domesticated dogs, which are descended from wolves, are good family pets. *(Job #7)*
   *The words **which are descended from wolves** are not needed.*

8. The landlord finally replaced the apartment's orange shag carpet. *(None)*
   *The adjectives **orange** and **shag** are not coordinate.*

9. The imitation paneling, however, will not be replaced until next year. *(Job #5)*

10. People who don't brush and floss have a much higher incidence of cavities. *(None)*
    *The words **who don't brush and floss** are needed in this sentence.*

Exercise 4.4 Advanced Commas

1. The patient walked into the cold, cramped waiting room. *(Job #6)*
   ***Cold** and **cramped** are coordinate.*

2. Abraham Lincoln, author of the Gettysburg Address, is considered one of America's greatest orators. *(Job #7)*
   The words in the middle are non-essential.

3. San Francisco, however, has a much cooler climate than Los Angeles. *(Job #5)*

4. The barista squirted heavy whipping cream onto the steaming vanilla latte. *(None)*
   ***Heavy** and **whipping** are not coordinate. **Steaming** and **vanilla** are not coordinate.*

5. During flu season we should all thank the person who invented the paper tissue. *(None)*
   *The words **who invented the paper tissue** are essential.*

6. The granite counter tops, a last minute addition, sent the new house over budget. *(Job #7)*
   The words in the middle are non-essential.

7. Roberto scanned the bleachers of the school's gym for his girl-friend, Jasmine, and her friends. *(Job #7)*

Assuming Roberto has only one girlfriend, her name is non-essential.

8. Consequently, the teacher suggested that Monica get an early start on writing her long, complicated research paper. *(Job #5 and #6)*
Long *and* **complicated** *are coordinate.*

9. The girl who brought a snake to school received two days of suspension. *(None)*
The words **who brought a snake to school** *are essential.*

10. The soft lights in the counselor's office, however, contrasted with her loud, bossy personality. *(Job #5 and #6)*
Loud *and* **bossy** *are coordinate.*

Exercise 4.5 Analyzing Comma Jobs

1. Benjamin Franklin was born in Boston, Massachusetts, but he later moved to Philadelphia, Pennsylvania. *(Job #3 and #2)*

2. Monkeys have tails, but gorillas do not have tails; they are both primates, however. *(Job #2 and #5)*

3. People who can't drive must take the bus, the train, or the subway. *(Job #1)*

4. While Gloria looked in the mirror, the hairdresser styled her long, beautiful hair. *(Job #4 and #6)*

5. Melissa's husband, Todd, likes to fish, hunt, and hike. *(Job #7 and #1)*

6. After hiking all day, Todd soaked his swollen, aching feet. *(Job #4 and #6)*

7. They met February 14, 2011, at a party, and they got married on February 14, 2012. *(Job #3 and #4)*

8. I had not planned to go out this evening; I could, however, be persuaded. *(Job #5)*

9. On the first day of kindergarten, Melissa watched her eldest daughter, Katie, get on the school bus. *(Job #4 and #7)*

10. Daniel washed the car, mowed the grass, and trimmed the bushes; consequently, his muscles were sore that evening. *(Job #1 and #5)*

Exercise 5.1 Apostrophes

1. The announcer's voice echoed throughout the stadium.
   The announcer owns his voice.
2. The Beatles first appeared on Ed Sullivan's variety show on August 24, 1964.
   The Beatles don't own anything. Ed Sullivan owns his show.
3. Jack Parr—Ed Sullivan's main rival—had aired footage of the Beatles in January 1964.
   Ed Sullivan "owns" his rival. The Beatles don't own anything.
4. The professor's car was towed because it was parked in the students' lot.
   The professor owns his/her car; the students own the parking lot.
5. Sam's cat's favorite game is clawing the drapes.
   Sam owns the cat; the cat owns its favorite game. (This is assuming that Sam has only one cat.)
6. The name Matthew means "God's gift," while Samantha's meaning is "God heard us."
   God owns the gift. Samantha owns the meaning.
7. England has had six kings named George.
   The kings don't own anything.
8. "Let's review for the test," announced the professor's assistant.
   ***Let's** is a contraction of **let us**. The professor "owns" the assistant.*
9. Graphing calculators are essential for students in upper-level math classes.
   The calculators don't own anything. The students don't own anything. The classes don't own anything.
10. Even though Frances owned a car, she had to borrow her roommate's car for trips over five miles.
    *No apostrophe is needed in **Frances** because of the wording of the sentence. An apostrophe would be needed if the sentence said **Frances' car**. The roommate owns her car. Trips and miles don't own anything.*

Exercise 5.2 Apostrophes

1. The author's previous lectures had been wildly successful.
   The author owns her lectures.
2. Six hundred people purchased their tickets months in advance to reserve their spots. *None*
   The tickets don't own anything. The spots don't own anything.
3. Early in the morning, the auditorium's air conditioning units malfunctioned.
   The auditorium owns the air conditioner
4. The program's producer called a repair crew.
   The program "owns" the producer.
5. When the repair techs arrived, they couldn't fix the air conditioners because they didn't have the right parts.
   Couldn't and **didn't** *are contractions. The air conditioners don't own anything. The parts don't own anything.*
6. Sweat dripped down the author's face as she began the lecture.
   The author owns her face.
7. Some paramedics arrived to treat a man who had fainted in the auditorium's stifling heat.
   The paramedics don't own anything. The auditorium owns the heat.
8. The author didn't want any lawsuits, so she stopped in the middle of the speech and asked the box office to refund the audience's money.
   Didn't *is a contraction. The audience owns its money.*
9. The people's impatience with the two employees trying to issue refunds created an even more unpleasant situation.
   The people own their impatience. The employees don't own anything. The refunds don't own anything.
10. When they left, everyone had experienced the author's message—global warming.
    The author owns her message.

Exercise 5.3 Plural Possessives

1. The **cats**' clawing pole is ragged. **more than one cat**
2. The **goose**'s honk was loud. **one goose**
3. The **student**'s work was correct. **one student**
4. The **women**'s restroom was crowded. **more than one woman**
5. The **birds**' nest was on a branch. **more than one bird**
6. The **squirrel**'s nest was in a tree. **one squirrel**
7. The **children**'s playroom was messy. **more than one child**
8. The **man**'s coat was warm. **one man**

Exercise 5.4 Capital Letters

1. For Christmas Aunt Josephine gave my mother a poodle named Ruffles.
   *Here the word **mother** is not capitalized because her first name cannot replace the family title.*
2. Many American companies have factories in other countries; for example, some Texas Instruments calculators are made in Utrecht, Netherlands.
   *The words **companies** and **countries** are general.*
3. Next Monday school will end at 11:30 so that the teachers can meet with parents while Superintendent Toni Godwin meets with the administrators.
   *The words **teachers, parents**, and **administrators** are general.*
   ***Superintendent** is a title coming before the person's name.*
4. Vincent D'Onofrio plays Robert Goren, one of TV's most fascinating detectives; his partner, Alex Eames, played by Kathryn Erbe, has been called the Dr. Watson to Goren's Sherlock Holmes.
5. Many English words have Spanish origins, including alligator, plaza, and stampede.

Exercise 5.5 Capitalization

1. We will go to Grandma's house for dinner.
2. My grandma makes great Christmas cookies.
3. For Thanksgiving Mom always bakes pumpkin pie.
4. My dad loves Thanksgiving because he likes to eat.
5. Miss Dixon went to Tokyo on her vacation.
6. Most of the people in Israel are Jewish.
7. On Wednesdays I go to my Spanish class.
8. Columbus sailed to America with the Nina, the Pinta, and the Santa Maria.
9. Many Asian people live in San Francisco.
10. We could go to an Italian restaurant, a Mexican restaurant, or a French restaurant.

Exercise 5.6 Colons, Dashes, and Semi-Colons

1. The most popular sports in America are football, basketball, and baseball.
   No additional punctuation is needed here. A colon after **are** *would be incorrect because the words which follow it are needed to finish the idea.*
2. America's most popular sports—football, basketball, and baseball—are viewed by millions every year.
   The long pauses provided by dashes are appropriate to set off the list of sports.
3. As an executive assistant for marketing, Jaime has traveled to three major international cities this year: Lima, Peru; Sydney, Australia; and Rome, Italy.
   The colon comes at the end of an independent clause and introduces a list. The semi-colons are needed in this list because the items in the list include commas.
4. Hillside High's Brad Pitt—no relation to the famous actor—has three favorite teachers: Mr. Smith, Mrs. Wilkins, and Ms. Cassidy.

The dashes provide a long pause to set off the extra information in the middle of the sentence. The colon comes at the end of an independent clause and introduces a list.

5. The week before Christmas, the malls are packed with people buying gifts; the week after Christmas, the malls are packed with people returning gifts.
   This is the classic use of a semi-colon to separate two independent clauses.

6. My old car got twelve miles per gallon; my new car gets thirty.
   The semi-colon separates two independent clauses.

7. Stefan—a true coffee snob—will only drink Starbuck's espresso.
   The dashes provide long pauses around the extra material in the middle of this sentence.

8. Only one thing kept me from flying to Acapulco for spring break: I didn't have any money.
   A semi-colon would be ok in this sentence because there are two independent clauses. A colon is a better choice because it gives a dramatic introduction to the completion of the sentence.

9. Jan spent her spring break in Acapulco; she went to Aspen for Christmas.
   The semi-colon separates two independent clauses. A colon would not work well here because the second clause is not really a completion of the idea given in the first clause.

10. When you're buying real estate, only three things matter: location, location, and location.
    The colon comes at the end of an independent clause and introduces a list.

Exercise 6.1 Pronoun Case

1. The first place prize in the school's robot contest went to Eric and (I – **me**).
2. Cecilia and (**I** – me) took turns driving home for Spring Break.
3. Mark invited (I – **me**) to play golf with (he – **him**) and Julian.

4. (**She** – Her) and Patty spent all day stripping wallpaper.
5. Be sure to call (we – **us**) as soon as you hear from (they – **them**).
6. (Him – **He**) and (her – **she**) have decided to go to Hawaii for their honeymoon.
7. I know (him – **he**) and (her – **she**) will have a wonderful trip.
8. Martha is coming over this afternoon to help Emily and (I – **me**) clean out the attic.
9. Nothing could have prepared (they – **them**) for the surprise when (**they** – them) won the lottery.
10. On Thanksgiving (**we** – us) all go to Grandma's house to eat the wonderful meal (her – **she**) and Grandpa have prepared.

Exercise 6.2 Pronoun Agreement

The antecedent is in bold type.

1. **Everybody** should pack (**his/her** – their) suitcase before going to breakfast.
2. **Sylvia and I** got an early start on (her – **our**) holiday shopping.
3. Both **Bill and Roger** installed satellite dishes on (his – **their**) roofs.
4. Neither Bill nor **Roger** fell off (**his** – their) roof.
5. **Two** of the boys forgot (his – **their**) backpack.
6. All **employees** must submit (his/her – **their**) expense reports by Friday.
7. **Someone** left (**her** – their) purse in the conference room.
8. Neither the professor nor the **students** could believe (his/her – **their**) eyes when the lab rat escaped.
9. **Anyone** who answers (**his/her** – their) cell phone during class will be counted absent.
10. **One** of the girls fell and skinned (**her** – their) knee.

Exercise 6.3 Pronoun Agreement

1. All students must pay (their) library fines by the end of the semester.
   *All students is plural, so the plural pronoun **their** matches.*
2. Both Sheila and Cindy got (their) hair done for graduation.
   *The antecedent is plural, **Sheila AND Cindy**.*
3. One of the students left (his/her) flash drive in the computer lab.
   One is singular, and the student could be male or female.
4. Everyone can pick up (his/her) paycheck on Friday.
   ***Everyone** is singular, and the employee could be male or female.*
5. Someone left (his) football helmet and pads in the locker room.
   ***Someone** is singular; **his** is okay here since all the football players are male.*
6. Three of the kids left (their) permission slips at home.
   ***Three** is plural, so **their** matches.*
7. Both Cody and Dustin were late for (their) 8:00 classes.
   *The antecedent is plural, **Cody AND Dustin.***
8. Neither Cody nor Dustin heard (his) alarm clock.
   *The antecedent is **Dustin** since his name is closest to the pronoun.*
9. Anyone who brings cookies to class will get extra credit on (his/her) quiz.
   ***Anyone** is singular, and the student could be male or female.*
10. Either the coach or the players will tell the newscaster (their) thoughts about the game.
    *The antecedent is **players** since that word is closest to the pronoun.*

Exercise 6.4 Subject–Verb Agreement

The subject is underlined.

1. <u>Jennifer and Nicole</u> (meets – **meet**) at the Suds-n-Bubbles Laundromat every Monday to wash their clothes.
2. Either Jennifer or <u>Nicole</u> (**brings** – bring) magazines to read while the clothes are washing.

3. <u>All</u> of Aunt Sadie's prize rose bushes (was – **were**) covered with aphids.
4. <u>One</u> of the rose bushes (**was** – were) still blooming, however.
5. Neither the employees nor the <u>manager</u> (**knows** – know) how to install a new roll of paper into the cash register.
6. <u>Red Lobster and Olive Garden</u> (are) my favorite restaurants.
7. Neither Red Lobster nor <u>Olive Garden</u> (takes) reservations.
   *Match the verb to **Olive Garden** since this is the name closest to it.*
8. <u>Olive Garden</u>, one of the best Italian restaurants, (serves) great spaghetti.
9. <u>Red Lobster</u>, which has a huge tank full of lobsters, (offers) fresh seafood.
10. Both <u>Red Lobster and Olive Garden</u> (have) wonderful desserts.

Exercise 6.5 Subject-Verb Agreement

1. <u>Megan and her friends</u> (work) at Starbucks.
2. Either Megan or her <u>friends</u> (take) orders from the customers.
   *Match the verb to **friends** since this is the word closest to the verb.*
3. Neither Megan nor the other <u>employees</u> (want) to take out the trash.
   *Match the verb to **employees** since this is the word closest to the verb.*
4. <u>Megan</u>, the newest of the employees, (has) to do this nasty job.
5. The <u>dumpster</u>, which is in an alley full of trash cans, (smells) terrible.
6. <u>Jasmine</u>, one of Megan's co-workers, (gives) Megan a sympathetic smile.
7. Before Megan got hired, <u>Jasmine</u> (was) the one taking out the trash.
8. <u>Megan and her friends</u> (enjoy) preparing the drinks.
9. The <u>coffee and tea</u> (smell) wonderful.
10. <u>One</u> of Megan's favorite drinks (is) a skinny mocha.

Exercise 7.1 Misplaced and Dangling Modifiers

1. I loaned my wool sweater to Jackie with the red stripes.
   This is a misplaced modifier; it sounds like Jackie has red stripes.
   I loaned my wool sweater with the red stripes to Jackie.
   OR I loaned Jackie my wool sweater with the red stripes.

2. To save electricity, remember to always turn down the thermostat when you leave the house.
   This sentence has a split infinitive.
   To save electricity, always remember to turn down the thermostat when you leave the house.
   OR To save electricity, always turn down the thermostat when you leave the house.

3. The museum curator showed the new painting to the guests hanging on the wall.
   This is a misplaced modifier; it sounds like the guests are hanging on the wall.
   The museum curator showed the new painting hanging on the wall to the guests.
   OR The museum curator showed the guests the new painting hanging on the wall.

4. Walking quickly, the convenience store is about ten minutes away.
   This is a dangling modifier; there is nobody in the sentence to walk quickly.
   Walking quickly, you can reach the convenience store in about ten minutes.
   OR The convenience store is about ten minutes away if you walk quickly.

5. The doctor suggested a new treatment for my ingrown toenail that is painless.
   This is a misplaced modifier; it sounds like the ingrown toenail is painless.
   The doctor suggested a new, painless treatment for my ingrown toenail.
   OR For my ingrown toenail, the doctor suggested a new treatment that is painless.

6. Patrick promised to never leave the milk out overnight again.
This is a split infinitive. Patrick promised never to leave the milk out overnight again.

7. Sara ordered a bagel from the waitress with cream cheese.
This is a misplaced modifier. It sounds like the waitress had cream cheese. Sara ordered a bagel with cream cheese from the waitress.

8. Eating tacos, the salsa dripped all over my hands.
This is a dangling modifier. Who is eating the tacos? When I was eating tacos, the salsa dripped all over my hands.

9. While studying for my history exam, my roommate turned on the tv.
This is a dangling modifier. Who is studying? It sounds like the roommate is studying. While I was studying for my history exam, my roommate turned on the tv.

10. The dentist told Kevin to always floss his teeth.
This is a split infinitive. The dentist told Kevin always to floss his teeth. OR The dentist told Kevin to floss his teeth every day.

Exercise 7.2 Passive Voice

1. Sandy ate the brownies.
2. Someone beheaded King Louis XVI in Paris in 1793.
3. George washed the dishes.
4. The pirate dug up the buried treasure.
5. A member of the committee released the incorrect statistics.
6. Someone found three priceless paintings in a storage unit.
7. The board approved the new construction project.
8. Someone had inspected the faulty valve two months earlier.
9. The ushers will take tickets.
10. Someone will release the new movie on October 1.

Exercise 7.3 Wordiness

This paragraph could be revised in many ways. Here is one example of a revision that eliminates the wordiness:
If a quick pull on the starting cord does not start the mower's engine, press the primer button several times and then try pulling the cord again.

Exercise 7.4 Parallel Structure

1. In the attic, I found a broken typewriter, an old suitcase, and a dusty doll house.
2. Scott was voted player of the year for his speed, concentration, and leadership.
3. Florida is a popular vacation spot because it has theme parks, beaches, and great weather.
4. Jan's new job pays well, has great benefits, and provides two weeks of vacation.

> *Other options are **gives** two weeks of vacation,*
> ***offers** two weeks of vacation, etc.*

5. The mouse ran across the kitchen floor, behind the refrigerator, and into a hole.
6. The movie was dramatic and exciting.
7. Patricia went to the grocery store, the dry cleaners, and the bank.
8. The library smelled like mildew, dust, and old books.
9. During spring break, Jake wants to go to the beach, eat lots of seafood, and get a tan.
10. The flight attendants were cheerful, friendly, and smiling.

Exercise 9.1 Analyzing Sentence Types

1. After Chelsea left, Jordan found himself bored and restless. **CX**
2. He spent several days watching TV and playing video games. **S**
3. Chelsea sent him pictures of the Globe Theatre and Big Ben, and he sent her pictures of his cactus and the empty basketball court. **CP**

4. One day Jordan walked the entire campus, discovering numerous new buildings. **S**

5. The next day he returned to the Career Center where he found job postings and internship opportunities. **CX**

6. Chelsea, meanwhile, sent pictures of the Eiffel Tower. **S**

7. When Jordan found a local company looking for an intern in their accounting department, he e-mailed to ask about the position; they immediately replied that they had a sudden opening. **CPX**

8. The previous intern left in disgrace after he spilled coffee on the computer. **CX**

9. Jordan spent the next six weeks as an intern. **S**

10. At the end of the summer, Chelsea had numerous adventures in Europe to share, and Jordan had an internship experience for his resume. **CP**

Exercise 9.2 Analyzing Sentence Types

1. Because they eat a lot of vegetation, elephants travel long distances. CX

2. In just one day, an average elephant will eat over three hundred pounds of vegetation. S

3. Elephants grow up to twelve feet tall, and they weigh up to fourteen hundred pounds. CP

4. Elephants have the largest brain of any animal; a typical elephant brain is four times as large as a human brain.

5. An elephant's trunk is very sensitive because it contains forty thousand muscles; an elephant can pick up a small coin with its trunk. CPX

6. Although predators will kill baby elephants, adult elephants are typically safe from all predators except humans. CX

7. Despite their reputation for never forgetting anything, elephants remember things only as well as other animals like cats and dogs. S

8. The white elephant gift originated in ancient Asia where ordinary elephants were common, but white elephants were rare. CPX

9. Since white <u>elephants</u> <u>were</u> sacred, the unlucky <u>owner</u> of a white elephant <u>had</u> to feed it special food and <u>welcome</u> the elephant's many visitors. CX

> *Although this sentence has three verbs, it has only two subjects, so it is CX, not CPX.*

10. <u>No one</u> <u>wanted</u> to receive a white elephant as a gift. S

Exercise 9.3 Tricky Sentence Types

1. <u>Zork</u> and <u>Zink</u> <u>were</u> aliens from the planet Zigland. **S**
2. <u>Because</u> <u>they</u> <u>were</u> scientists, <u>they</u> <u>wanted</u> to visit Earth, so <u>they</u> <u>traveled</u> nearly a billion miles. **CPX**
3. <u>When</u> <u>they</u> <u>landed</u> on Earth, <u>they</u> <u>were</u> astonished by the colors. **CX**
4. On Zigland the <u>grass</u> <u>is</u> purple, and the <u>sky</u> <u>looks</u> yellow. **CP**
5. After climbing down from their space ship, <u>Zork</u> and <u>Zink</u> <u>went</u> exploring. **S**
6. <u>They</u> <u>gathered</u> plant specimens and <u>took</u> water samples. **S**
7. <u>Although</u> <u>they</u> <u>wanted</u> to interview some animals, <u>they</u> <u>failed</u> to make sense of the animals' noises. **CX**
8. <u>Since</u> <u>Zork</u> and <u>Zink</u> <u>were</u> the size of mice, a stray <u>cat</u> <u>chased</u> and <u>cornered</u> them; <u>she</u> <u>hoped</u> for a new lunch meat. **CPX**
9. The tiny <u>scientists</u> immediately <u>beamed</u> themselves back to their ship and <u>took</u> off for Zigland. **S**
10. After returning to Zigland with their samples, <u>they</u> <u>received</u> a hero's welcome. **S**

Answers and Explanations for Exercises 10.1, 10.2, 10.4, 10.5, and 10.6 are given in the text.

Exercise 10.3 Punctuating Quotations

When Joan Didion profiled artist Georgia O'Keefe, she noted that "O'Keefe is neither crusty nor eccentric. She is simply hard, a straight shooter, a woman clean of received wisdom and open to what she sees."

Explanation: Even if you are quoting more than one sentence, you don't need to put quotation marks at the end of one sentence and the beginning of the next sentence. Just keep going until the end of the quoted material.

"An old wife, an old dog, and ready money," says Franklin, "are three faithful friends."

Explanation: Here quotation marks are needed to show where the student's own words (says Franklin) interrupt the quoted material.

The counselor quoted Ben Franklin to the couple: "Keep your eyes wide open before marriage," but keep them "half shut afterwards."

Explanation: Be very precise about putting quotation marks around the words copied from the original.

Ralph Waldo Emerson writes, "The ancient precept 'Know Thyself' and the modern precept 'Study Nature' become at last one maxim."

Explanation: Use a capital letter to begin the quotation since this word was capitalized in the original. Use single quote marks to show the words that were in quote marks in the original. Put the period inside the closing quotation mark.

Will Rogers said, "I never met a man I didn't like."

Explanation: When you quote, copy all the words exactly. Put the period inside the closing quotation mark.

Exercise 10.7 Works Cited Listings

Write a Works Cited listing and a parenthesis for each of these sources:

Winchester, Simon. *The Professor and the Madman.* New York: Harper Collins, 1998. Print.

(Winchester 88)

Halpin, Anne and Betty Mackey. *Cutting Gardens.* New York: Simon and
    Shuster, 1993. Print.

(Halpin and Mackey 58–60)

Wagner, Eric. "Way of the Wolverine." *Smithsonian.* Jan. 2012: 13–15.

(Wagner 14)

Eligon, John. "In East Africa, Towns Suffer in Crackdown on Diamonds."
    New York Times 6 Jan. 2012: A4+. Print

(Eligon A8)

"Election Chief will not Resign." *New York Times* 6 Jan. 2012: A9. Print.

("Election" A9)

"Man, Isle of." *The Columbia Encyclopedia* 5th ed. Print.

("Man")

Cody, David. "Dickens: A Brief Biography." *The Victorian Web: Literature,
    History, and Culture in the Age of Victoria.* N.p. Mar. 2004. Web. 27
    Dec. 2011.

(Cody)

Index

Index